Days Like This

Days Like This™

Written by
J. Torres

Illustrated by
Scott Chantler

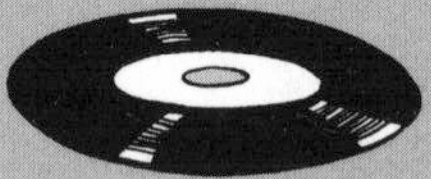

book design by
Keith Wood

edited by
Jamie S. Rich

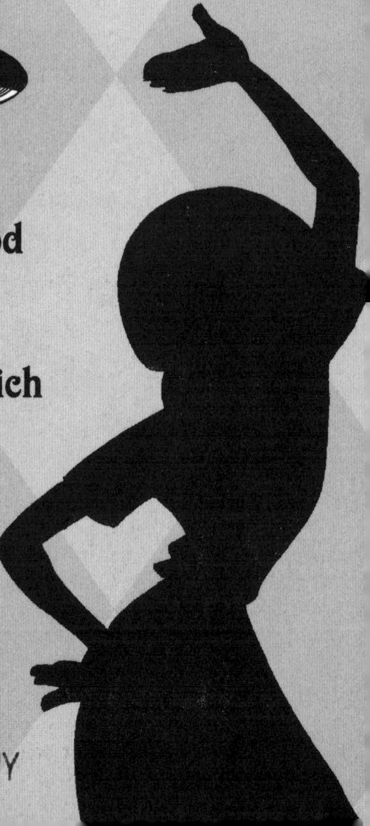

Oni Press

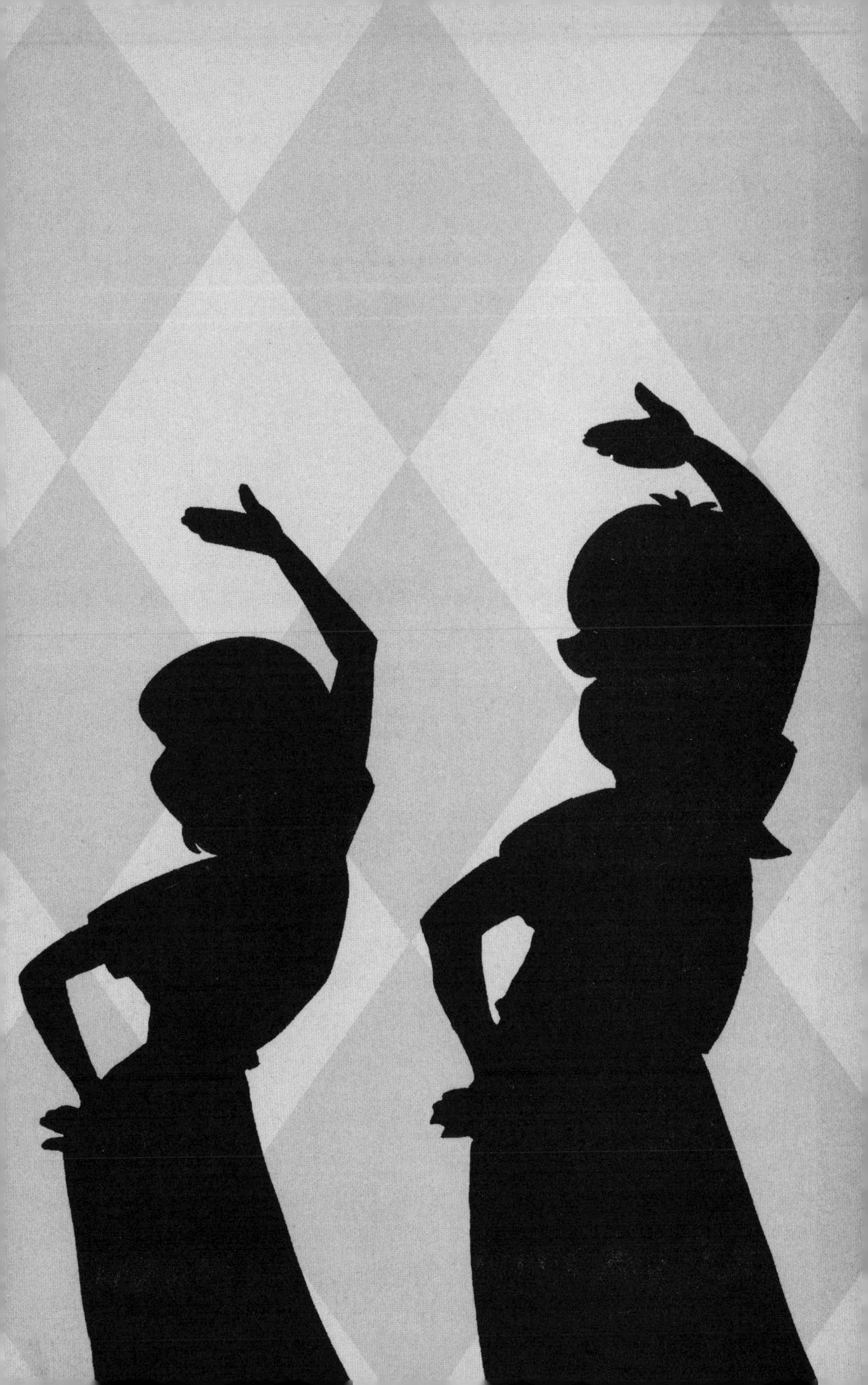

published by

Joe Nozemack

associate editing by

James Lucas Jones

Visit the author at *www.jtorresonline.com*.
Visit the illustrator at *www.scottchantler.com*.

ONI PRESS, INC.
6336 SE Milwaukie Avenue, PMB30
Portland, OR 97202
USA

www.onipress.com

First edition: March 2003
ISBN 1-929998-48-1

1 3 5 7 9 10 8 6 4 2
PRINTED IN CANADA

In loving memory of Renato Torres
(1939-2001)

"To know him is to love him."

CHAPTER 1
"Will You Still Love Me Tomorrow?"

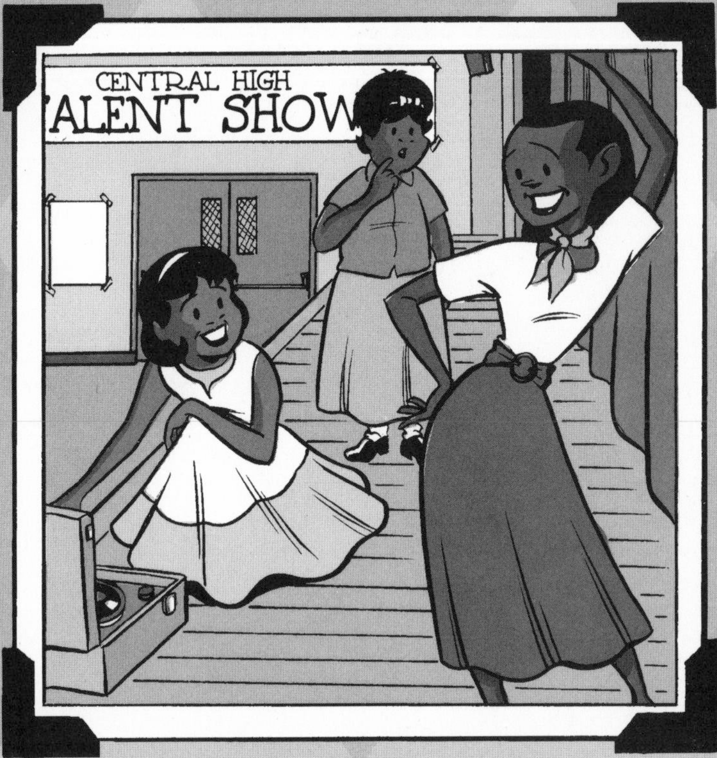
CENTRAL HIGH
TALENT SHOW

"Central High auditorium. Rehearsing for the talent show."

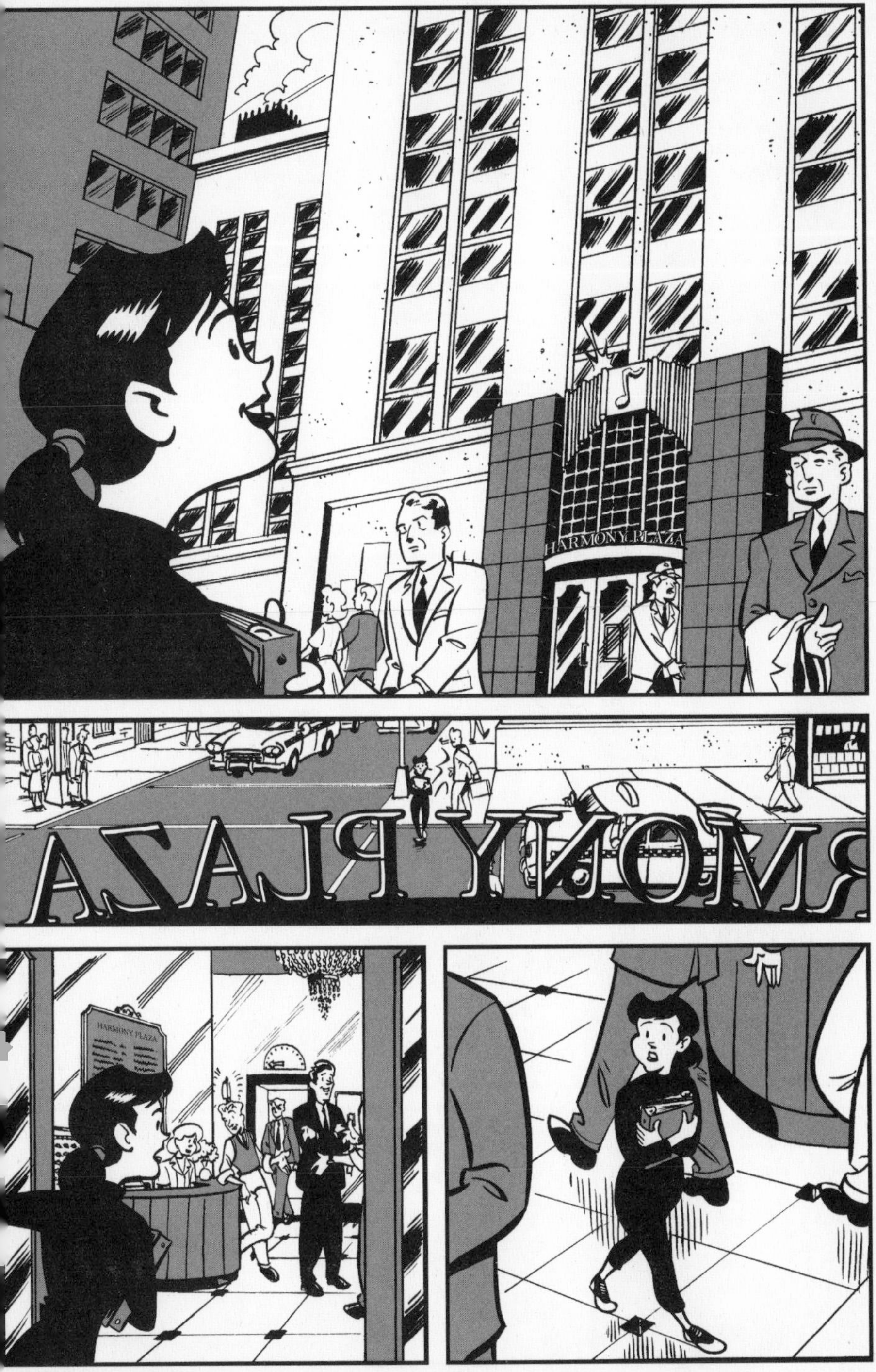
HARMONY PLAZA
RMONY PLAZA
HARMONY PLAZA

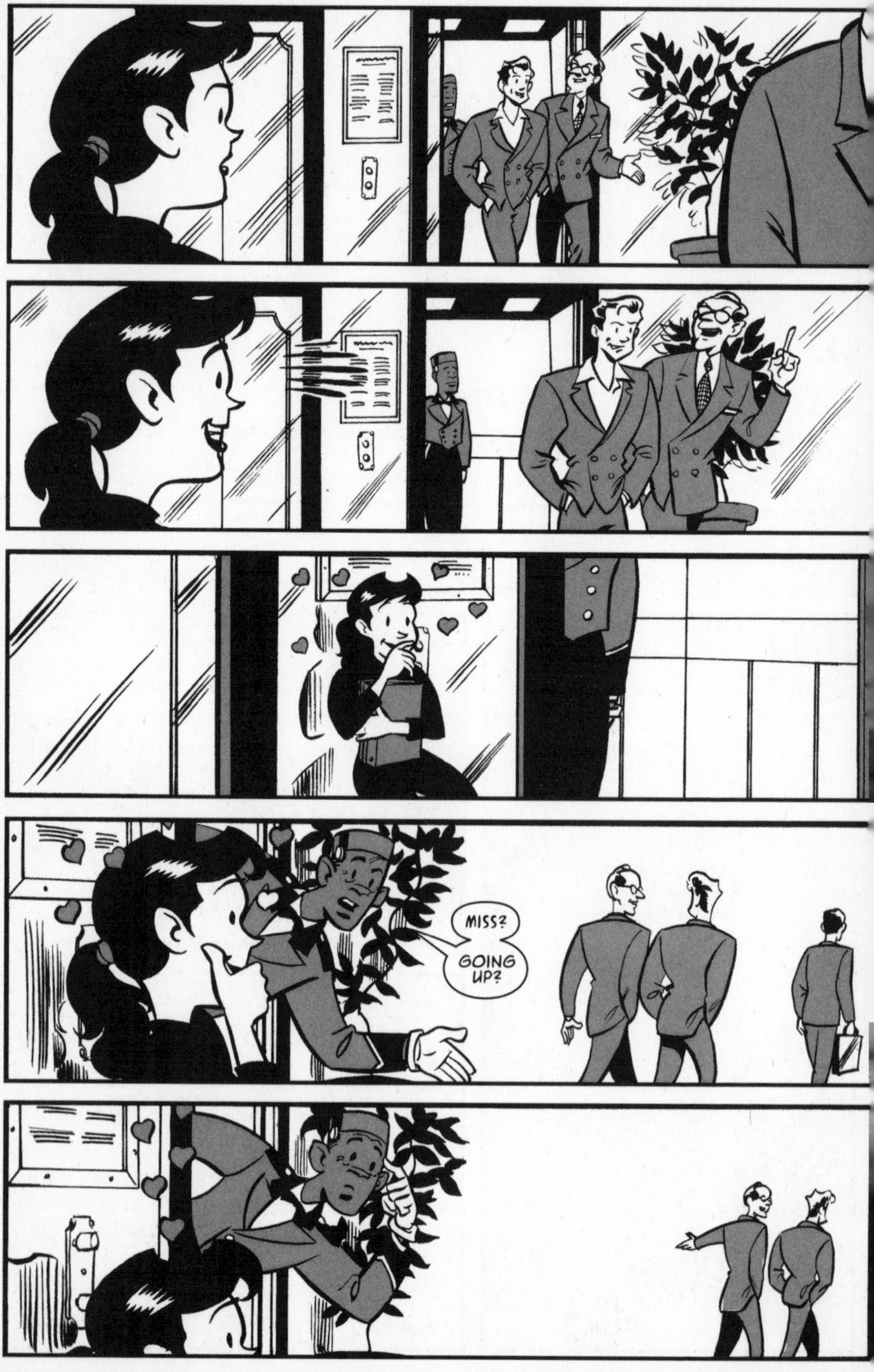
MISS?
GOING UP?

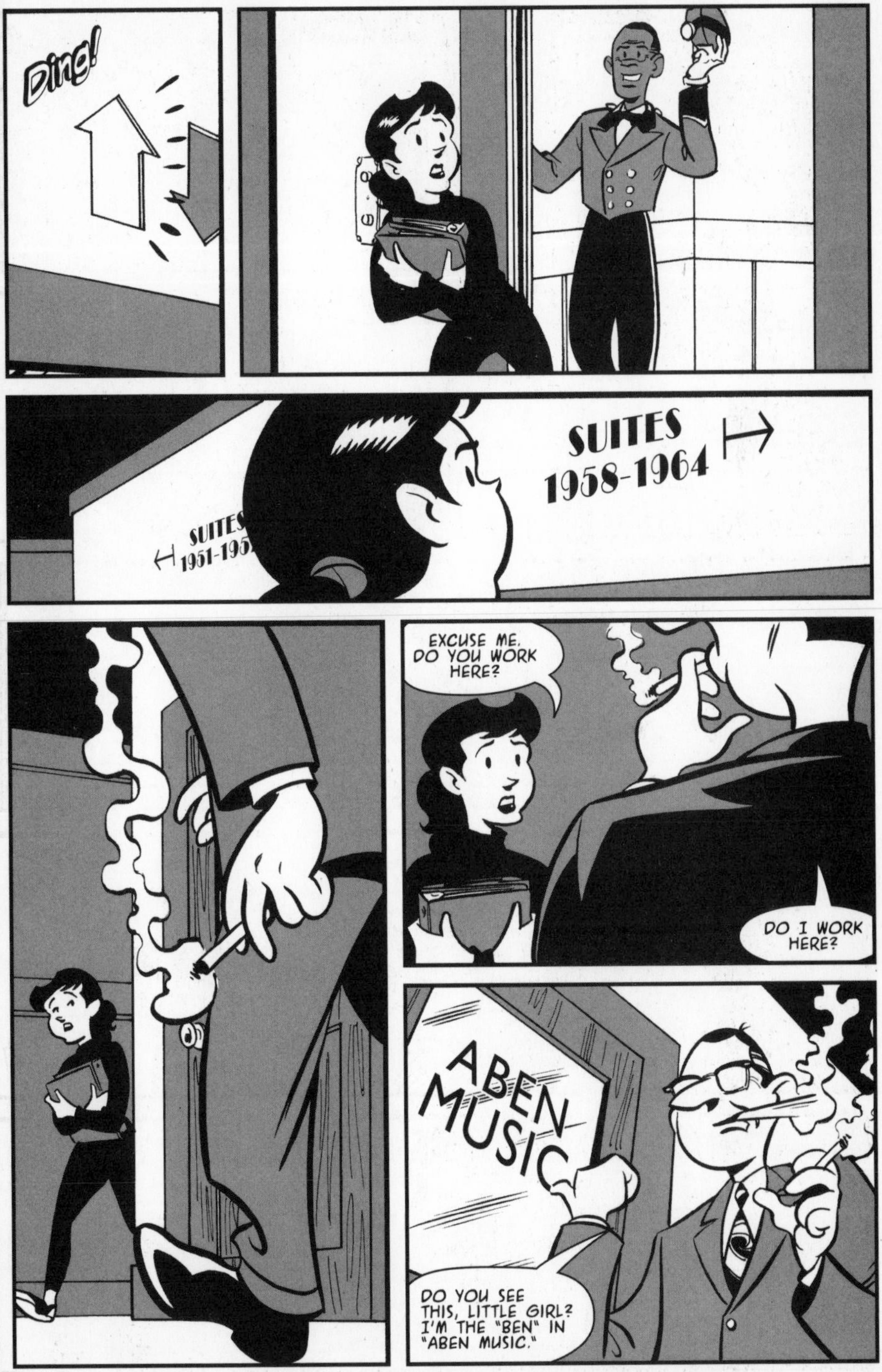
Ding!
SUITES
1958-1964
SUITES
1951-1957
EXCUSE ME. DO YOU WORK HERE?
DO I WORK HERE?
ABEN MUSIC
DO YOU SEE THIS, LITTLE GIRL? I'M THE "BEN" IN "ABEN MUSIC."

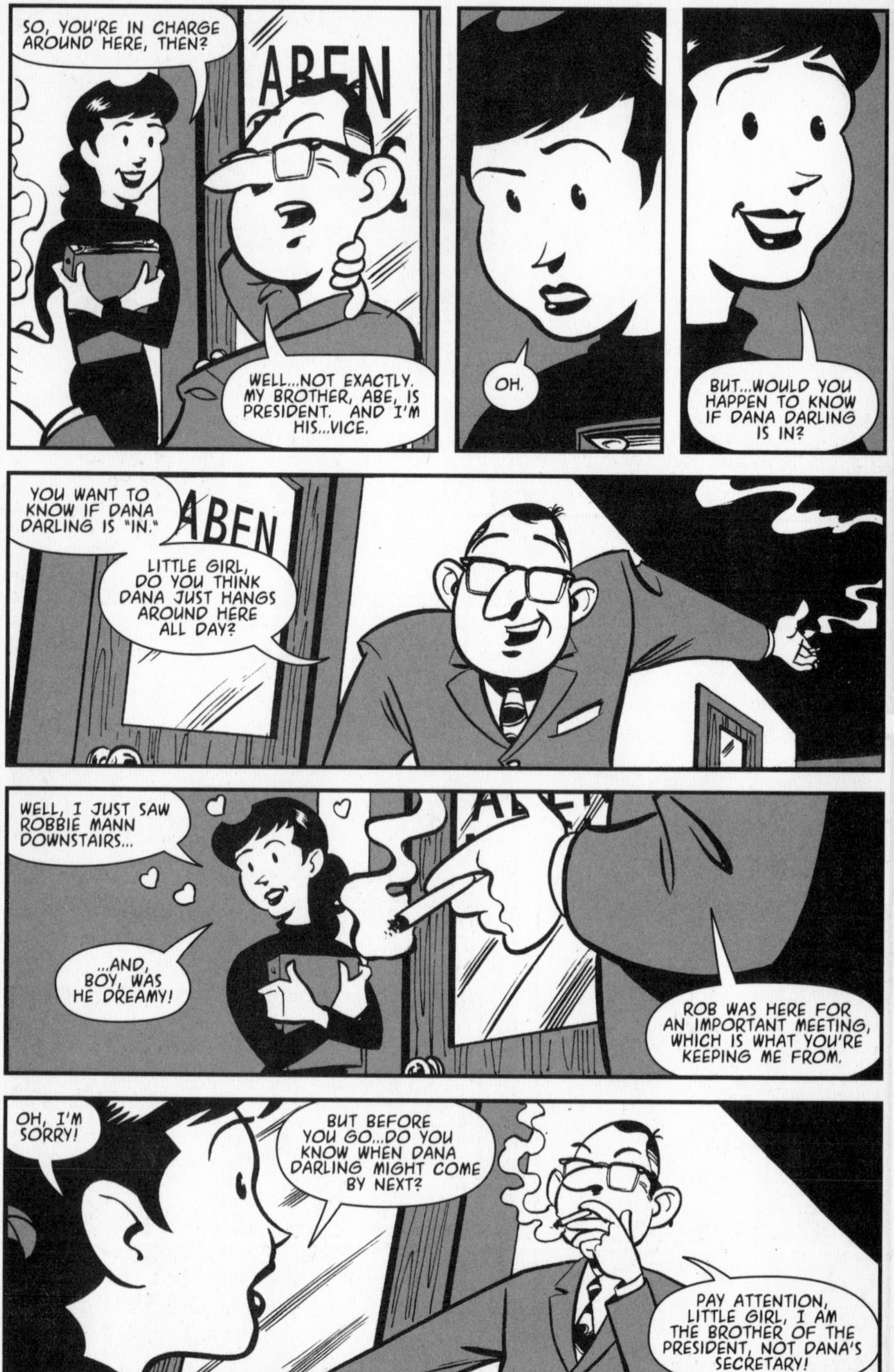

SO, YOU'RE IN CHARGE AROUND HERE, THEN?
ABEN
WELL...NOT EXACTLY. MY BROTHER, ABE, IS PRESIDENT. AND I'M HIS...VICE.
OH.
BUT...WOULD YOU HAPPEN TO KNOW IF DANA DARLING IS IN?
YOU WANT TO KNOW IF DANA DARLING IS "IN."
ABEN
LITTLE GIRL, DO YOU THINK DANA JUST HANGS AROUND HERE ALL DAY?
WELL, I JUST SAW ROBBIE MANN DOWNSTAIRS...
...AND, BOY, WAS HE DREAMY!
ROB WAS HERE FOR AN IMPORTANT MEETING, WHICH IS WHAT YOU'RE KEEPING ME FROM.
OH, I'M SORRY!
BUT BEFORE YOU GO...DO YOU KNOW WHEN DANA DARLING MIGHT COME BY NEXT?
PAY ATTENTION, LITTLE GIRL, I AM THE BROTHER OF THE PRESIDENT, NOT DANA'S SECRETARY!

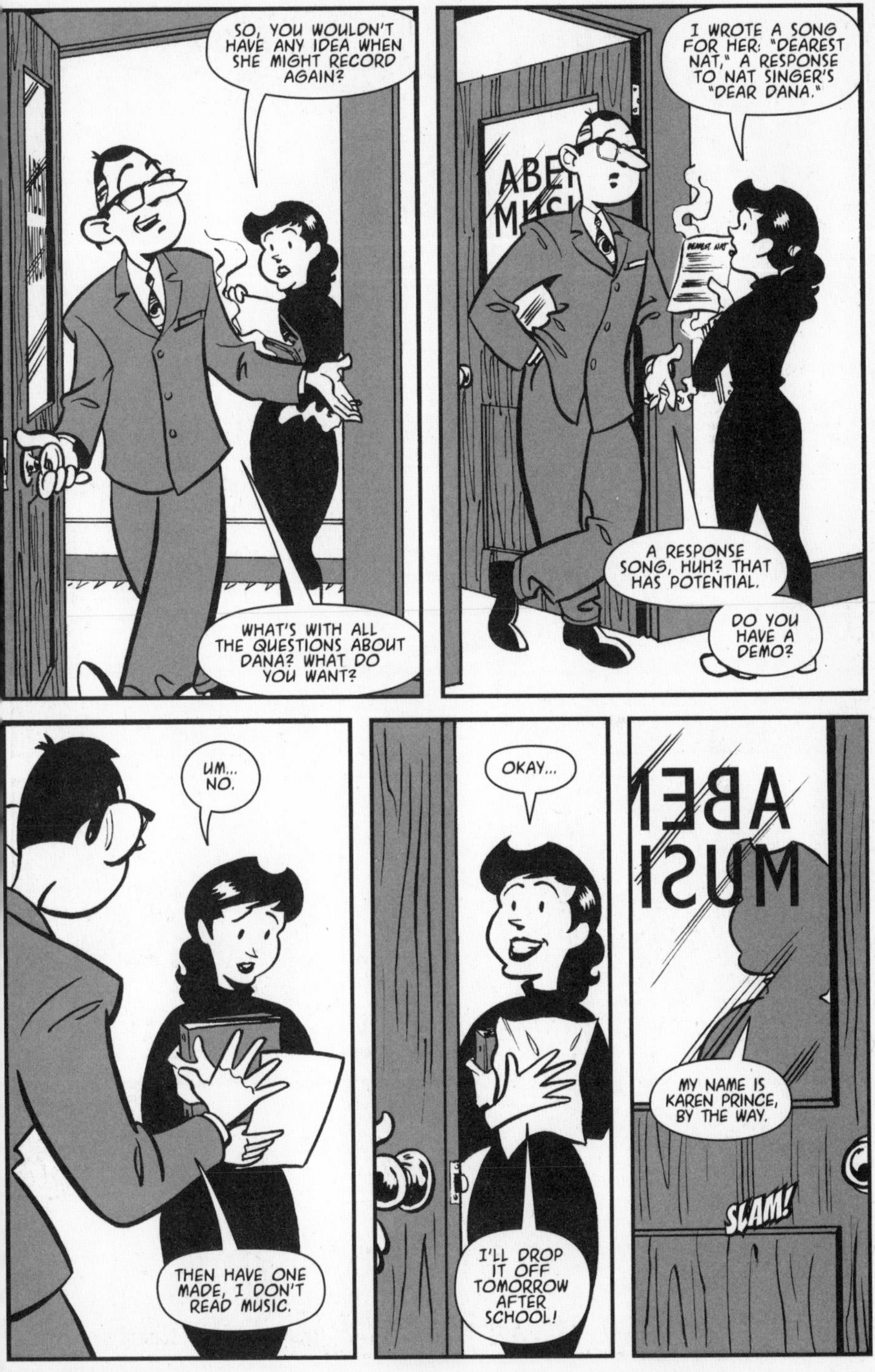
SO, YOU WOULDN'T HAVE ANY IDEA WHEN SHE MIGHT RECORD AGAIN?
WHAT'S WITH ALL THE QUESTIONS ABOUT DANA? WHAT DO YOU WANT?
I WROTE A SONG FOR HER: "DEAREST NAT," A RESPONSE TO NAT SINGER'S "DEAR DANA."
DEAREST NAT
A RESPONSE SONG, HUH? THAT HAS POTENTIAL.
DO YOU HAVE A DEMO?
UM... NO.
THEN HAVE ONE MADE, I DON'T READ MUSIC.
OKAY...
I'LL DROP IT OFF TOMORROW AFTER SCHOOL!
MY NAME IS KAREN PRINCE, BY THE WAY.
SLAM!

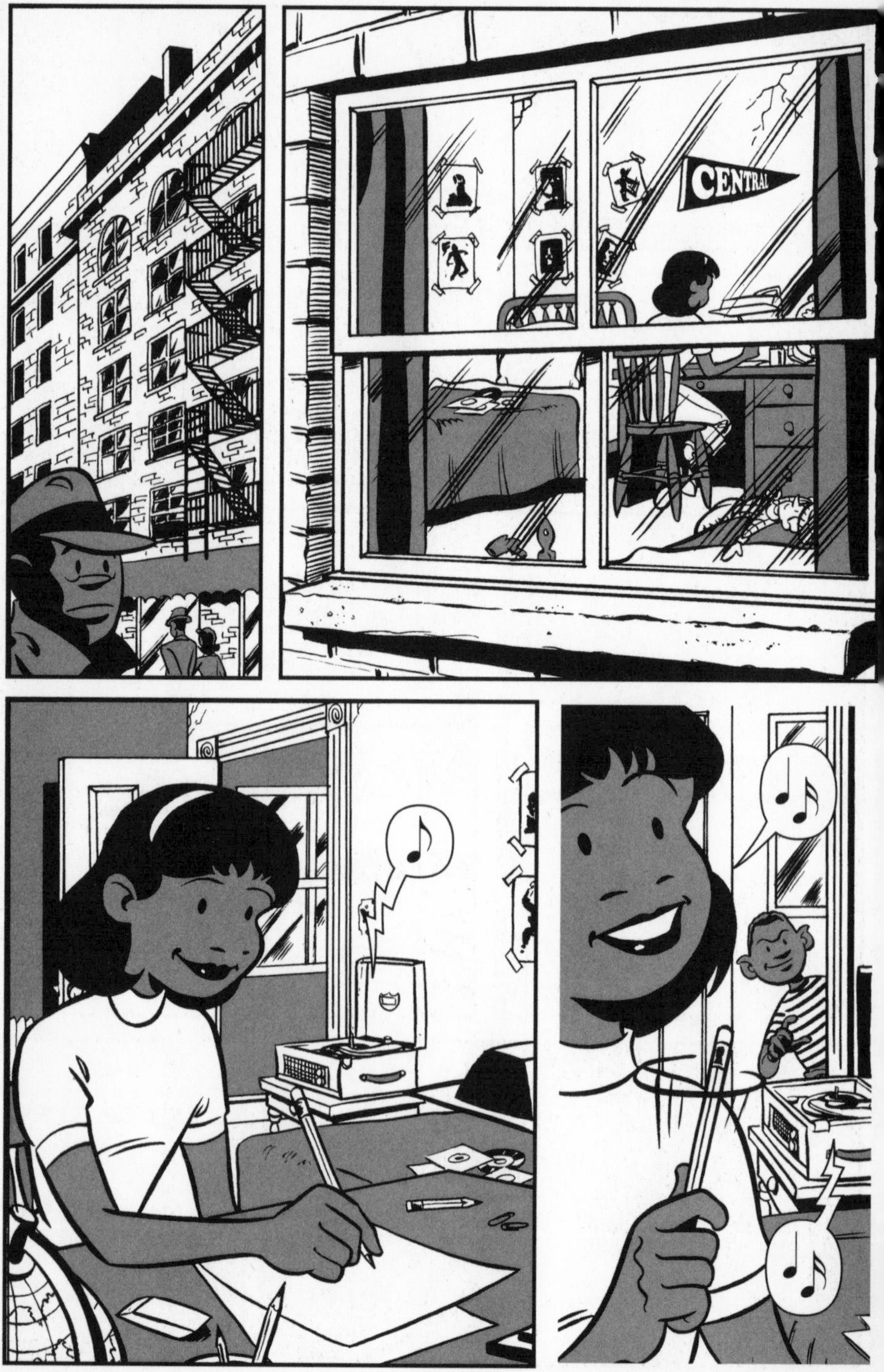
CENTRAL

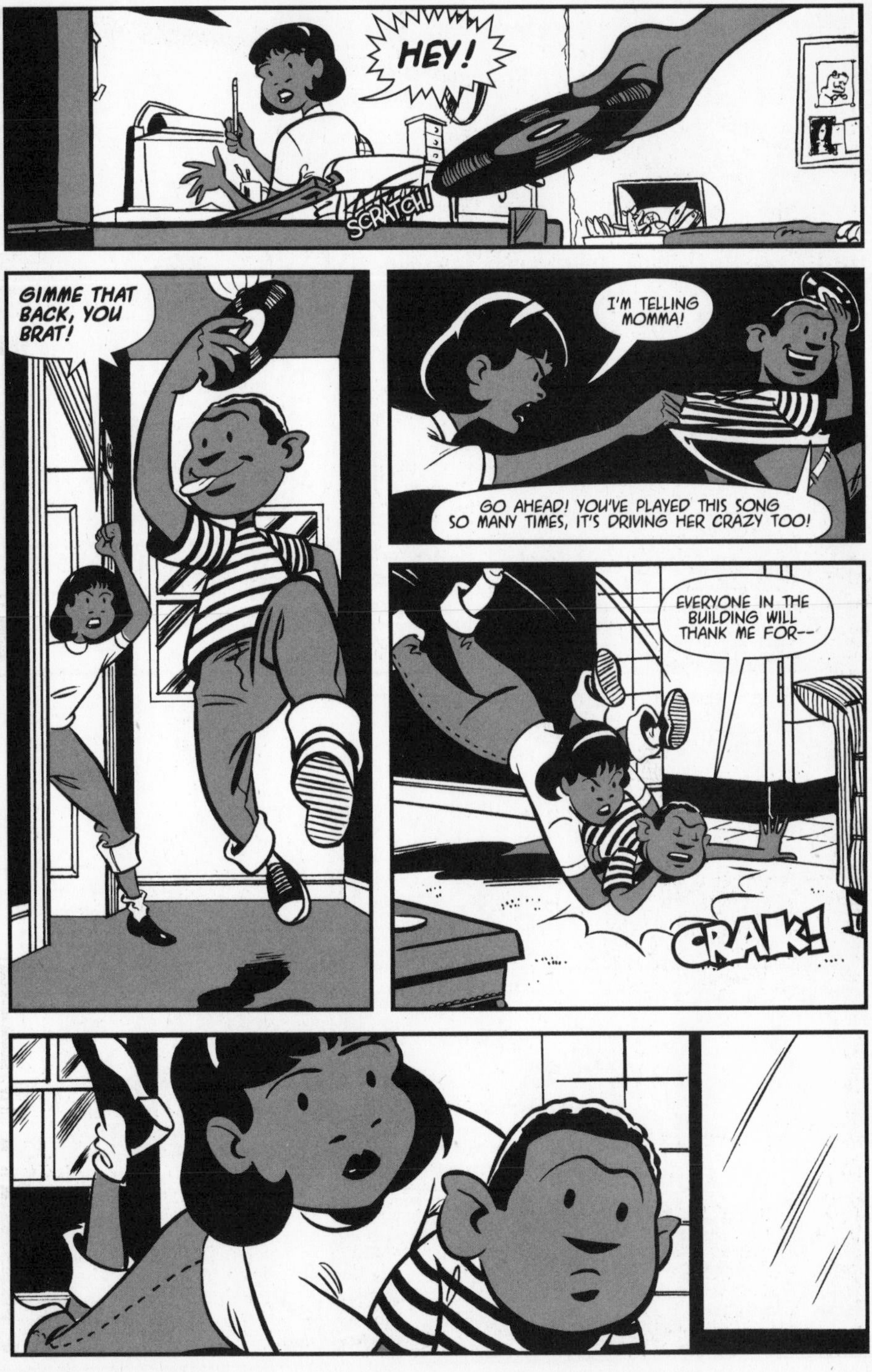
HEY!
SCRATCH!
GIMME THAT BACK, YOU BRAT!
I'M TELLING MOMMA!
GO AHEAD! YOU'VE PLAYED THIS SONG SO MANY TIMES, IT'S DRIVING HER CRAZY TOO!
EVERYONE IN THE BUILDING WILL THANK ME FOR--
CRAK!

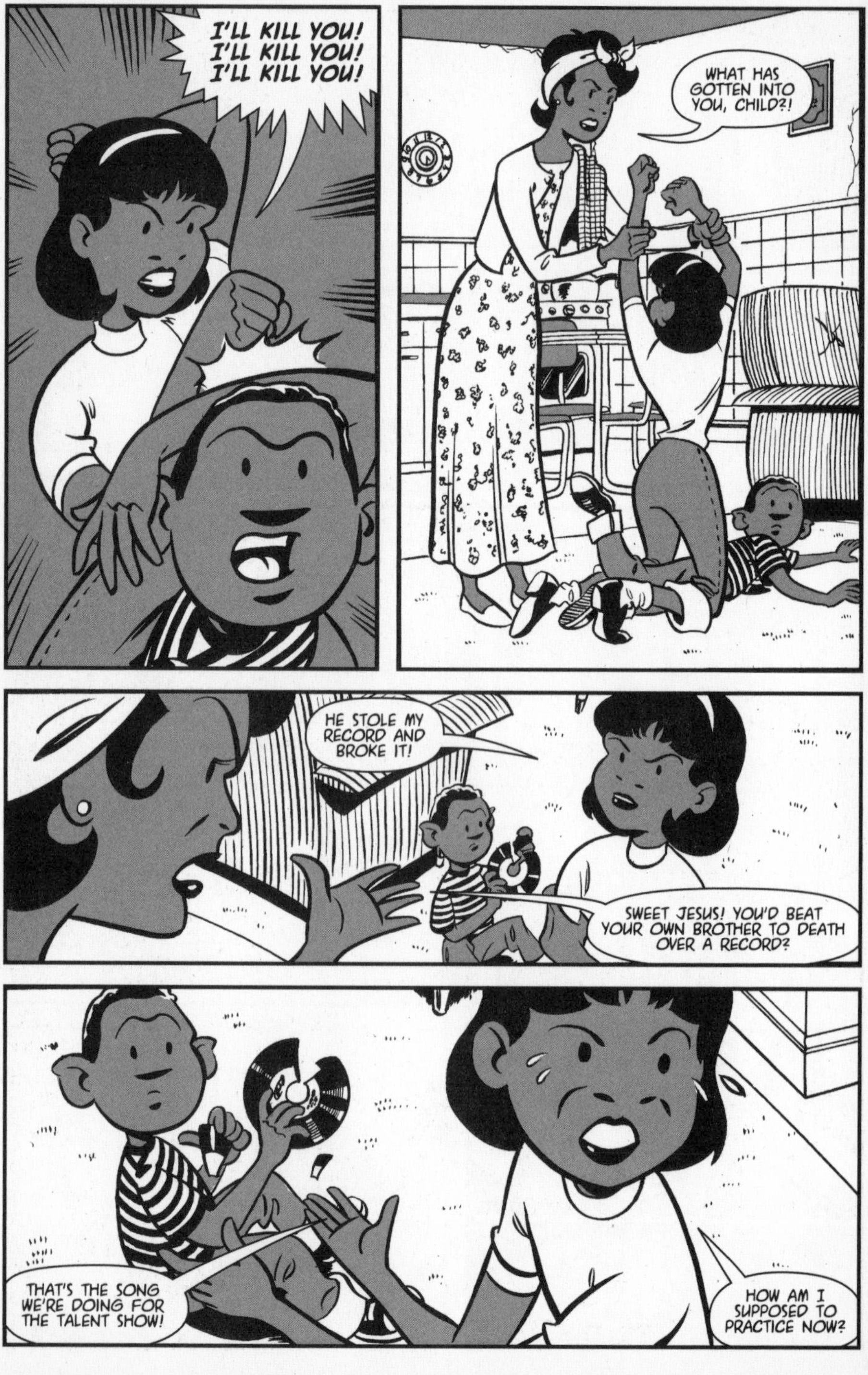
I'LL KILL YOU! I'LL KILL YOU! I'LL KILL YOU!
WHAT HAS GOTTEN INTO YOU, CHILD?!
HE STOLE MY RECORD AND BROKE IT!
SWEET JESUS! YOU'D BEAT YOUR OWN BROTHER TO DEATH OVER A RECORD?
THAT'S THE SONG WE'RE DOING FOR THE TALENT SHOW!
HOW AM I SUPPOSED TO PRACTICE NOW?

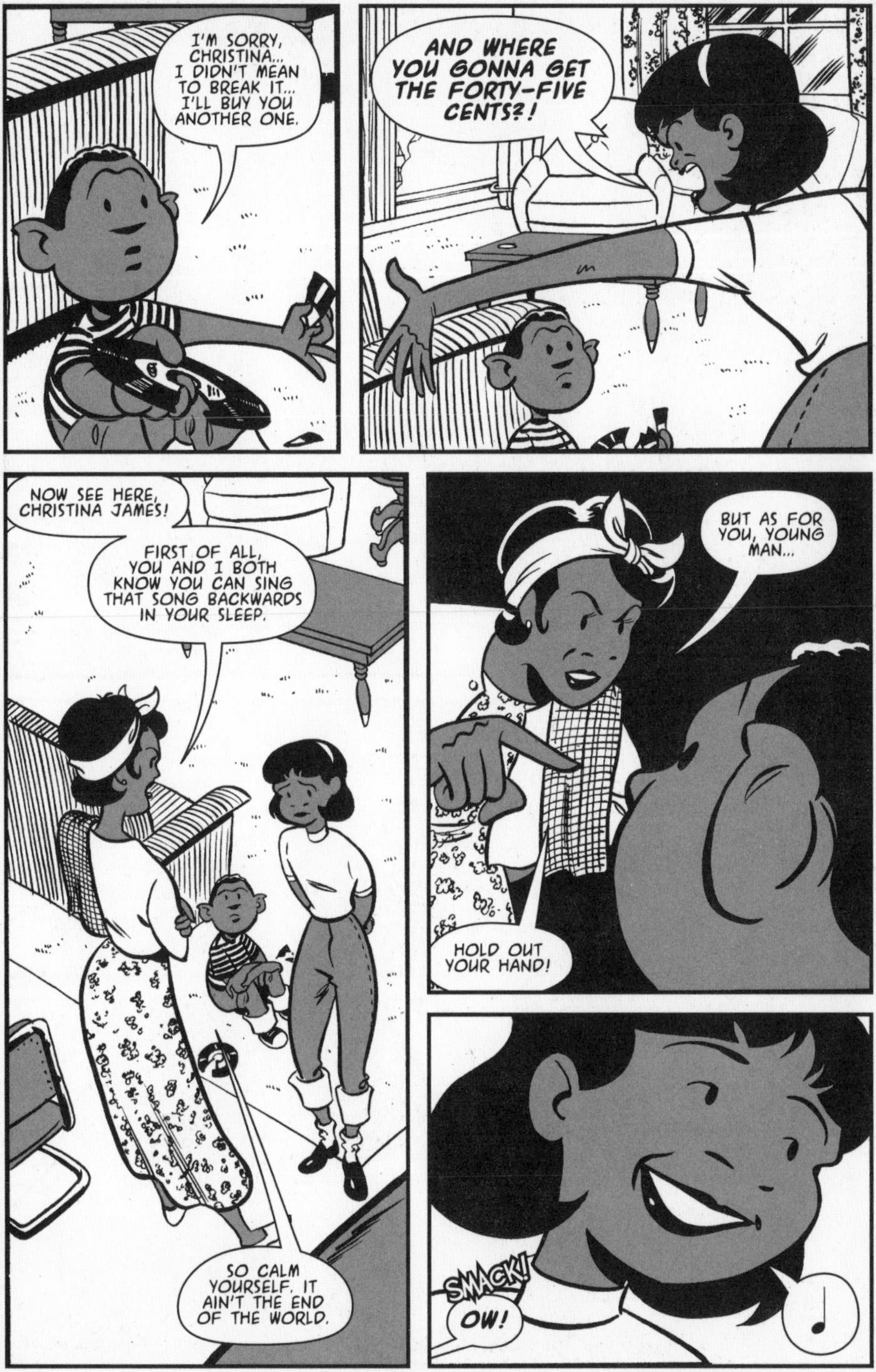
I'M SORRY, CHRISTINA... I DIDN'T MEAN TO BREAK IT... I'LL BUY YOU ANOTHER ONE.
AND WHERE YOU GONNA GET THE FORTY-FIVE CENTS?!
NOW SEE HERE, CHRISTINA JAMES!
FIRST OF ALL, YOU AND I BOTH KNOW YOU CAN SING THAT SONG BACKWARDS IN YOUR SLEEP.
SO CALM YOURSELF. IT AIN'T THE END OF THE WORLD.
BUT AS FOR YOU, YOUNG MAN...
HOLD OUT YOUR HAND!
SMACK!
OW!

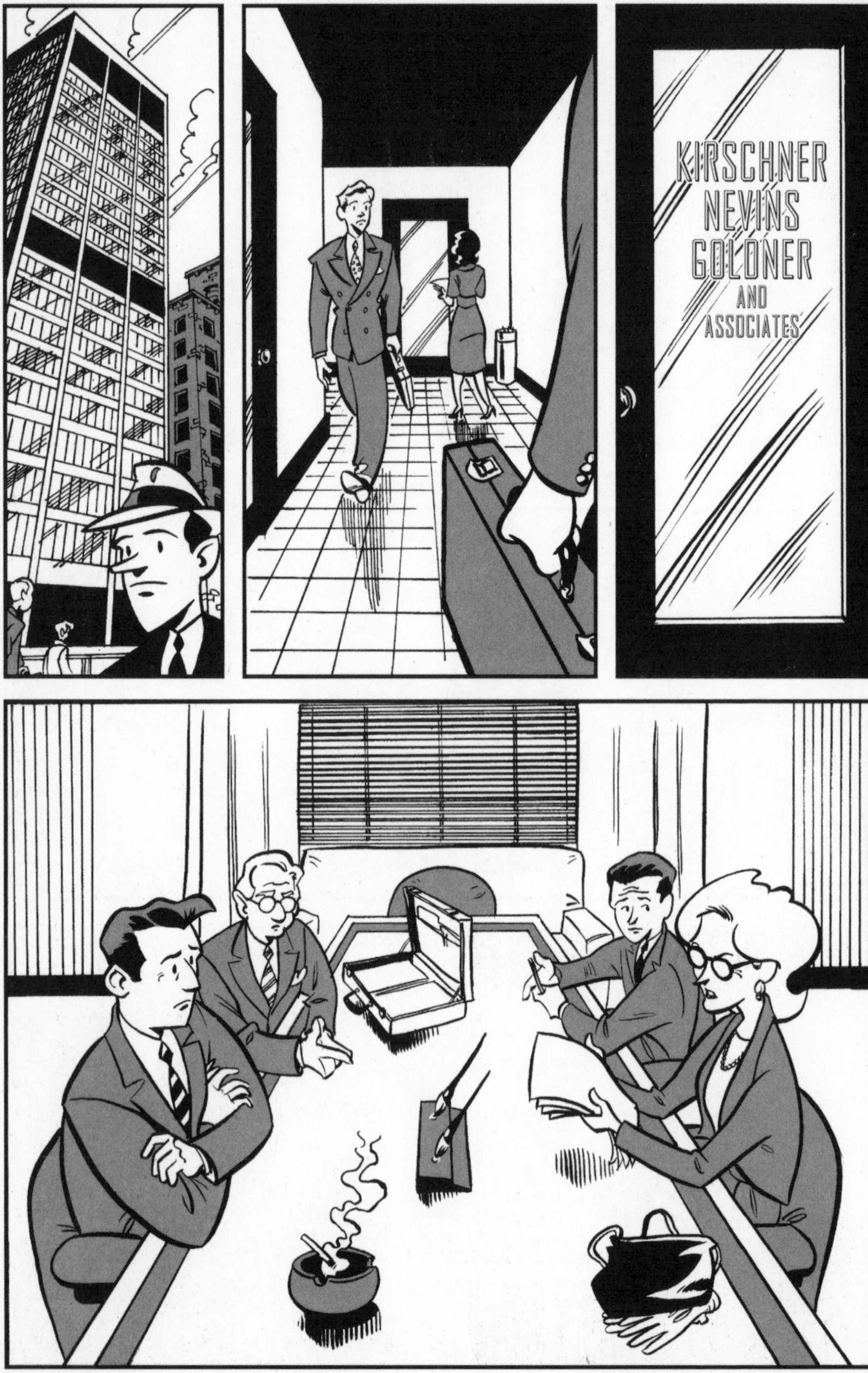
KIRSCHNER
NEVINS
GOLDNER
AND
ASSOCIATES

BY SIGNING THIS AGREEMENT YOU RELINQUISH ANY CLAIMS TO ABEN MUSIC, ITS PUBLISHING COMPANIES AND RECORD LABELS.

BUT AS YOU CAN SEE, ALL YOUR TERMS AS PER OUR LAST ROUND OF NEGOTIATIONS ARE IN THERE.

of the
ll claims court,
greement shall be
g arbitration
thics Committee or
ed upon arbitrator.
's award shall be final,
nt may be entered in,
having jurisdiction thereof.
t shall pay all arbitration
rt costs, reasonable
ey's fees, and legal interest on
award of judgement in favour of
na Solomon.

x Anna Solomon

ANNA...

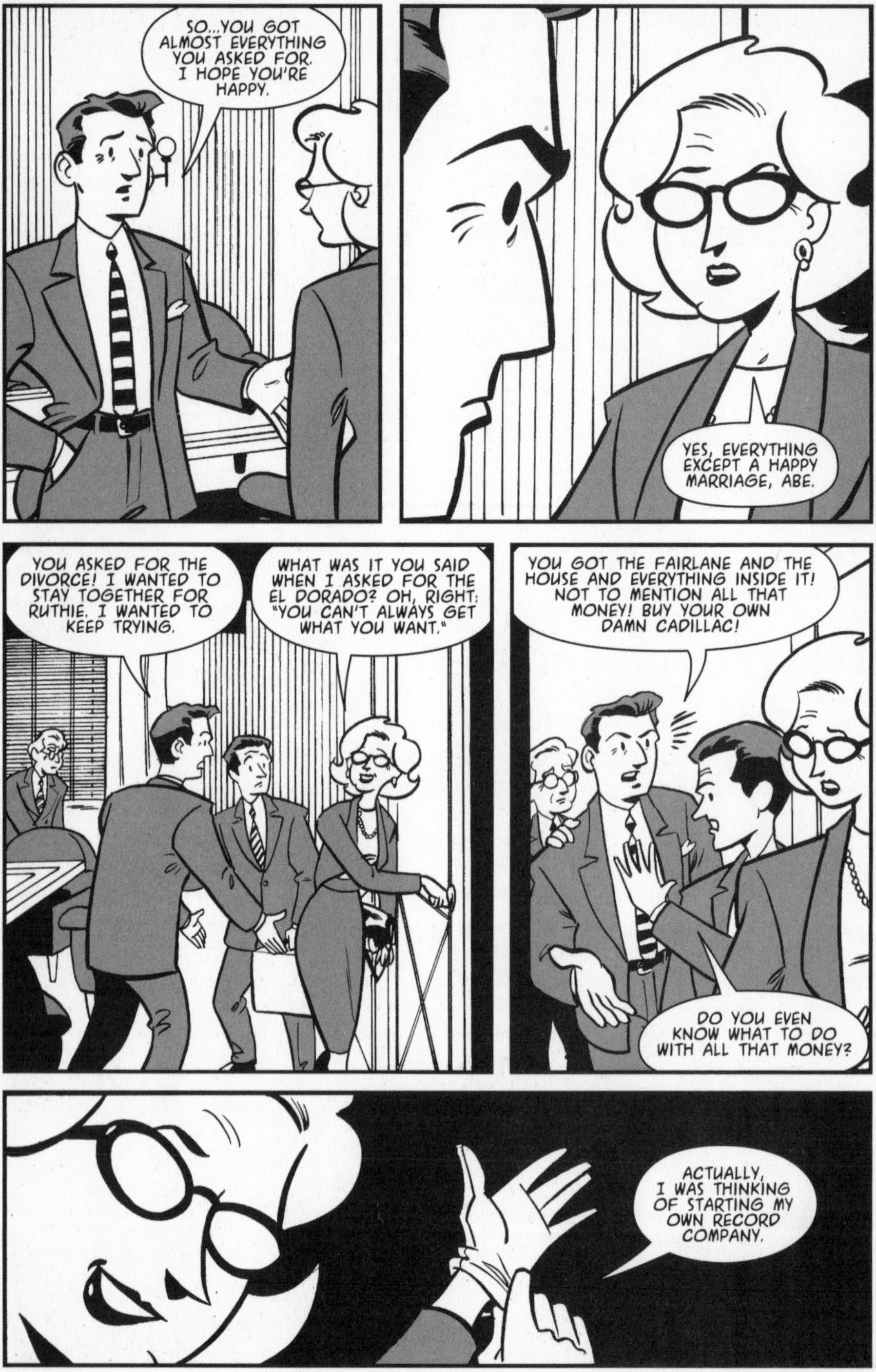
SO...YOU GOT ALMOST EVERYTHING YOU ASKED FOR. I HOPE YOU'RE HAPPY.
YES, EVERYTHING EXCEPT A HAPPY MARRIAGE, ABE.
YOU ASKED FOR THE DIVORCE! I WANTED TO STAY TOGETHER FOR RUTHIE. I WANTED TO KEEP TRYING.
WHAT WAS IT YOU SAID WHEN I ASKED FOR THE EL DORADO? OH, RIGHT: "YOU CAN'T ALWAYS GET WHAT YOU WANT."
YOU GOT THE FAIRLANE AND THE HOUSE AND EVERYTHING INSIDE IT! NOT TO MENTION ALL THAT MONEY! BUY YOUR OWN DAMN CADILLAC!
DO YOU EVEN KNOW WHAT TO DO WITH ALL THAT MONEY?
ACTUALLY, I WAS THINKING OF STARTING MY OWN RECORD COMPANY.

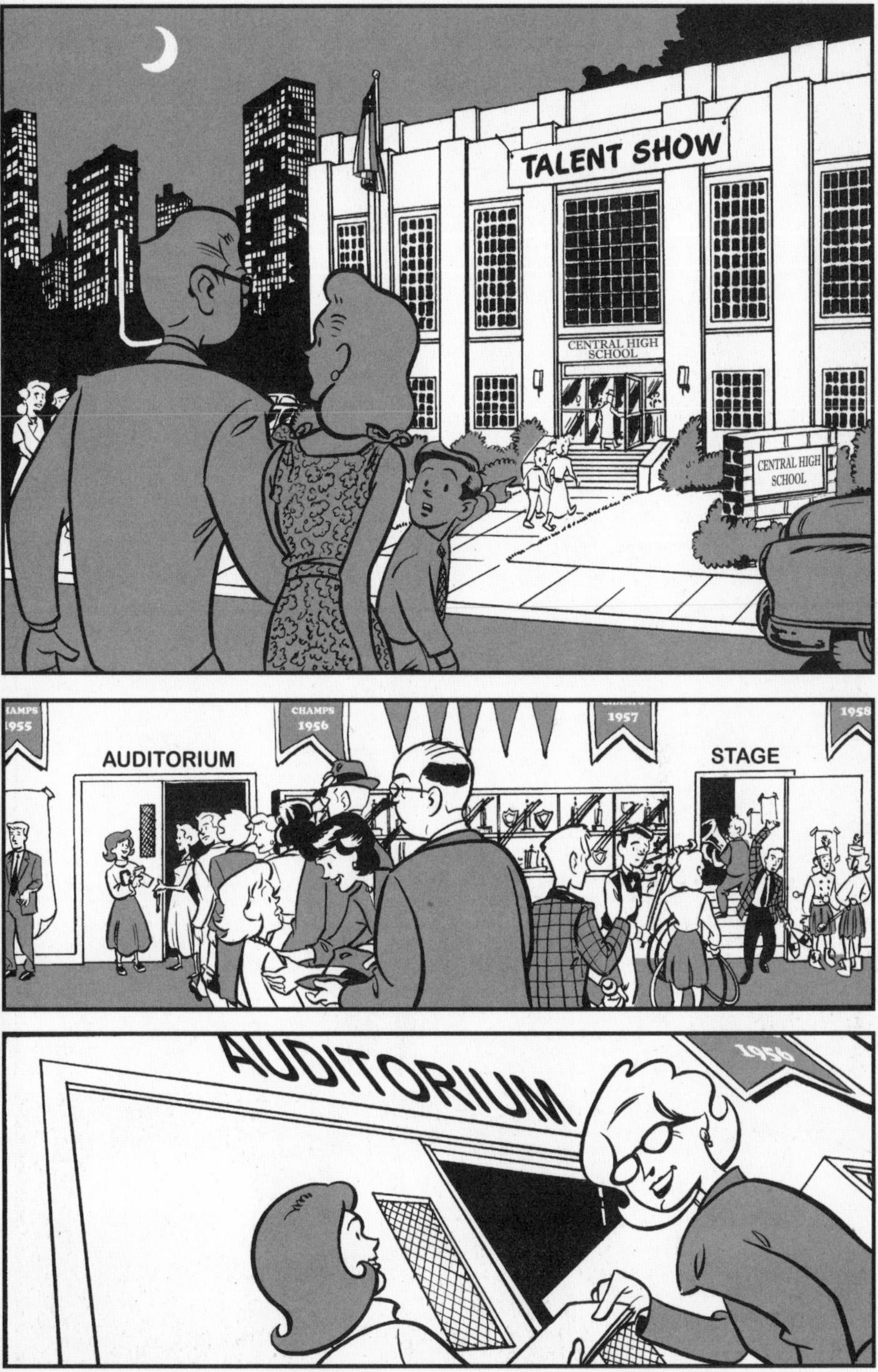
TALENT SHOW
CENTRAL HIGH SCHOOL
CENTRAL HIGH SCHOOL
CHAMPS 1956
1957
1958
AUDITORIUM
STAGE
AUDITORIUM
1956

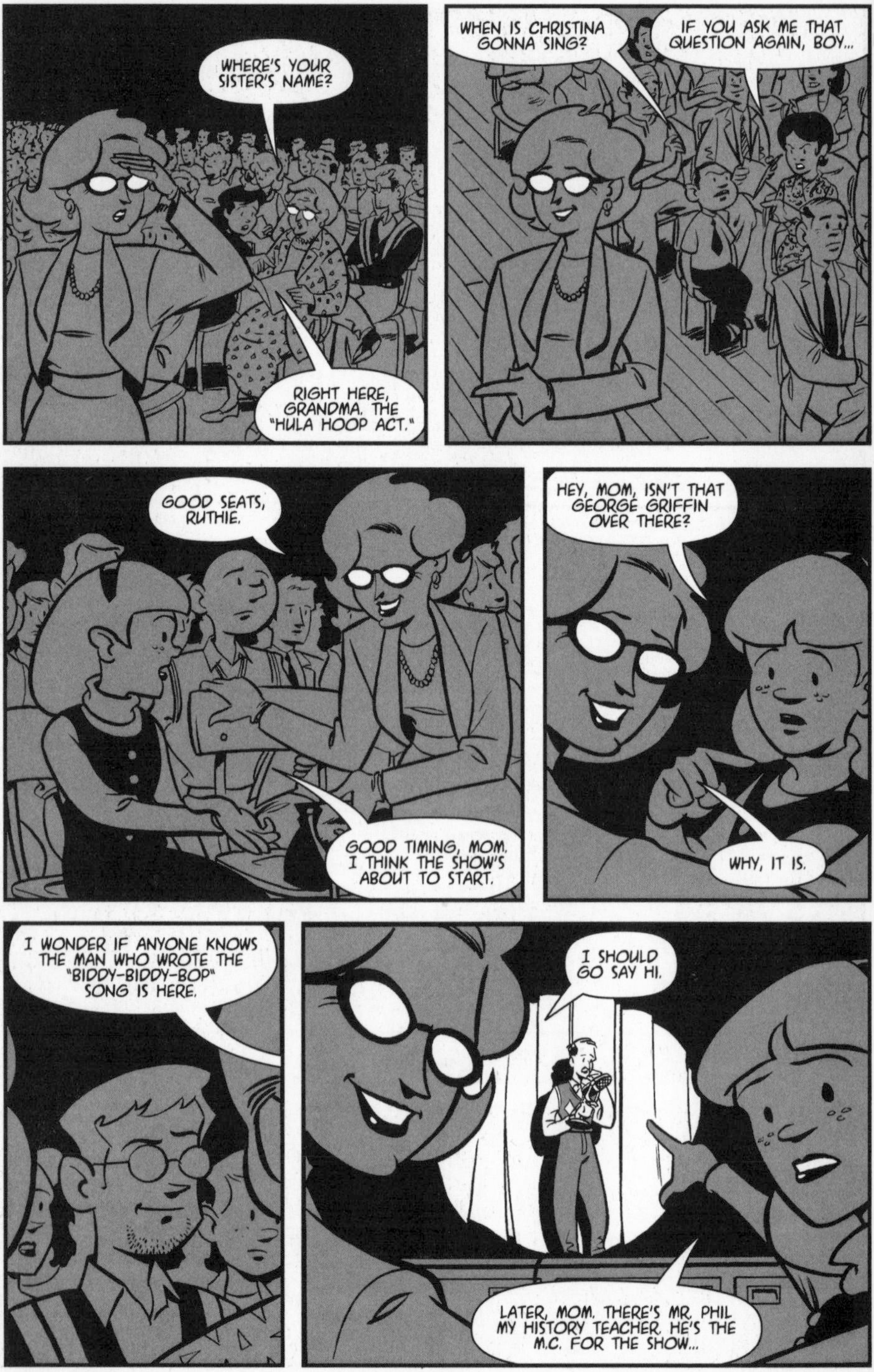
WHERE'S YOUR SISTER'S NAME?
RIGHT HERE, GRANDMA. THE "HULA HOOP ACT."
WHEN IS CHRISTINA GONNA SING?
IF YOU ASK ME THAT QUESTION AGAIN, BOY...
GOOD SEATS, RUTHIE.
GOOD TIMING, MOM. I THINK THE SHOW'S ABOUT TO START.
HEY, MOM, ISN'T THAT GEORGE GRIFFIN OVER THERE?
WHY, IT IS.
I WONDER IF ANYONE KNOWS THE MAN WHO WROTE THE "BIDDY-BIDDY-BOP" SONG IS HERE.
I SHOULD GO SAY HI.
LATER, MOM. THERE'S MR. PHIL MY HISTORY TEACHER. HE'S THE M.C. FOR THE SHOW...

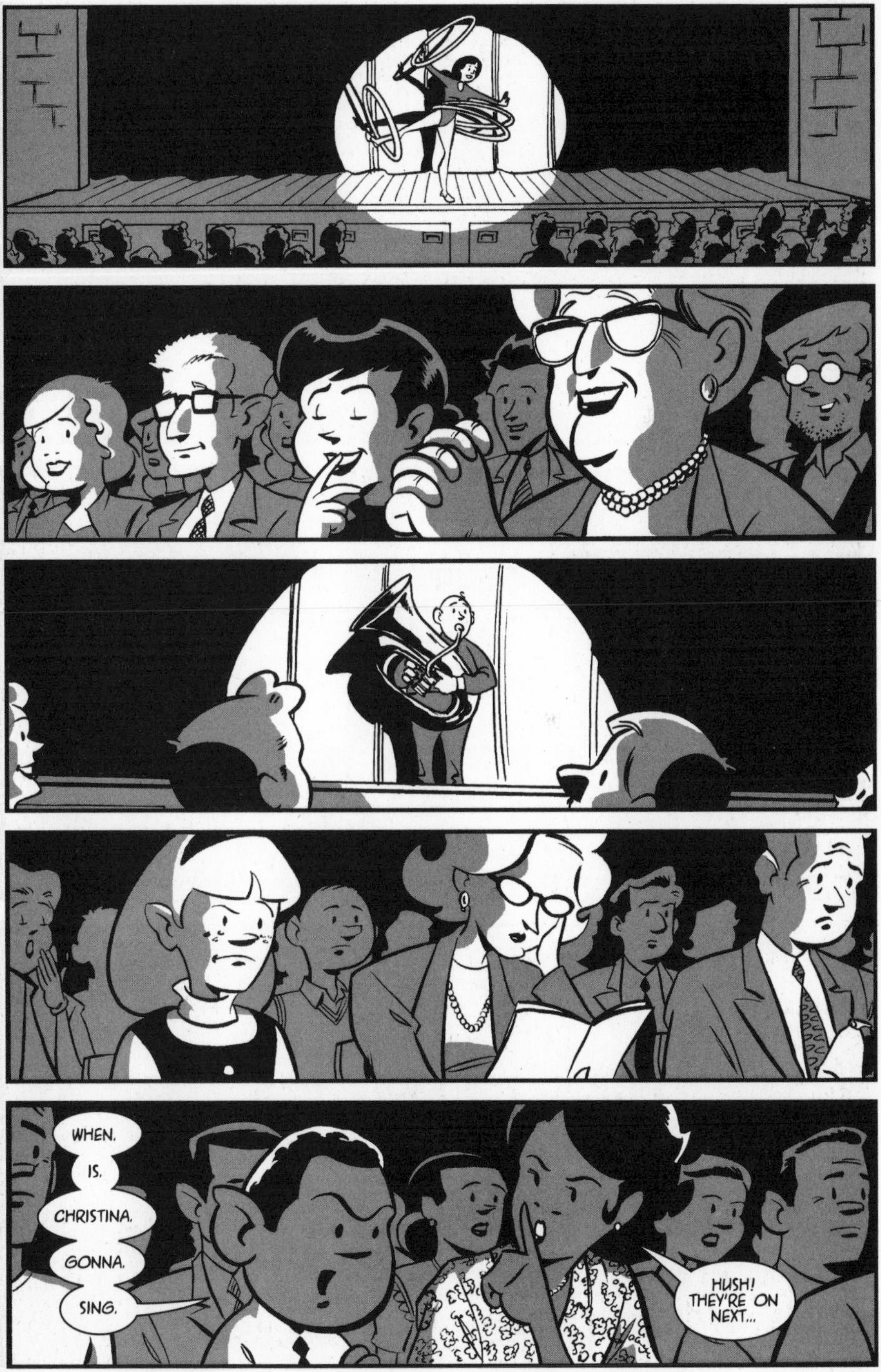
WHEN.
IS.
CHRISTINA.
GONNA.
SING.
HUSH! THEY'RE ON NEXT...

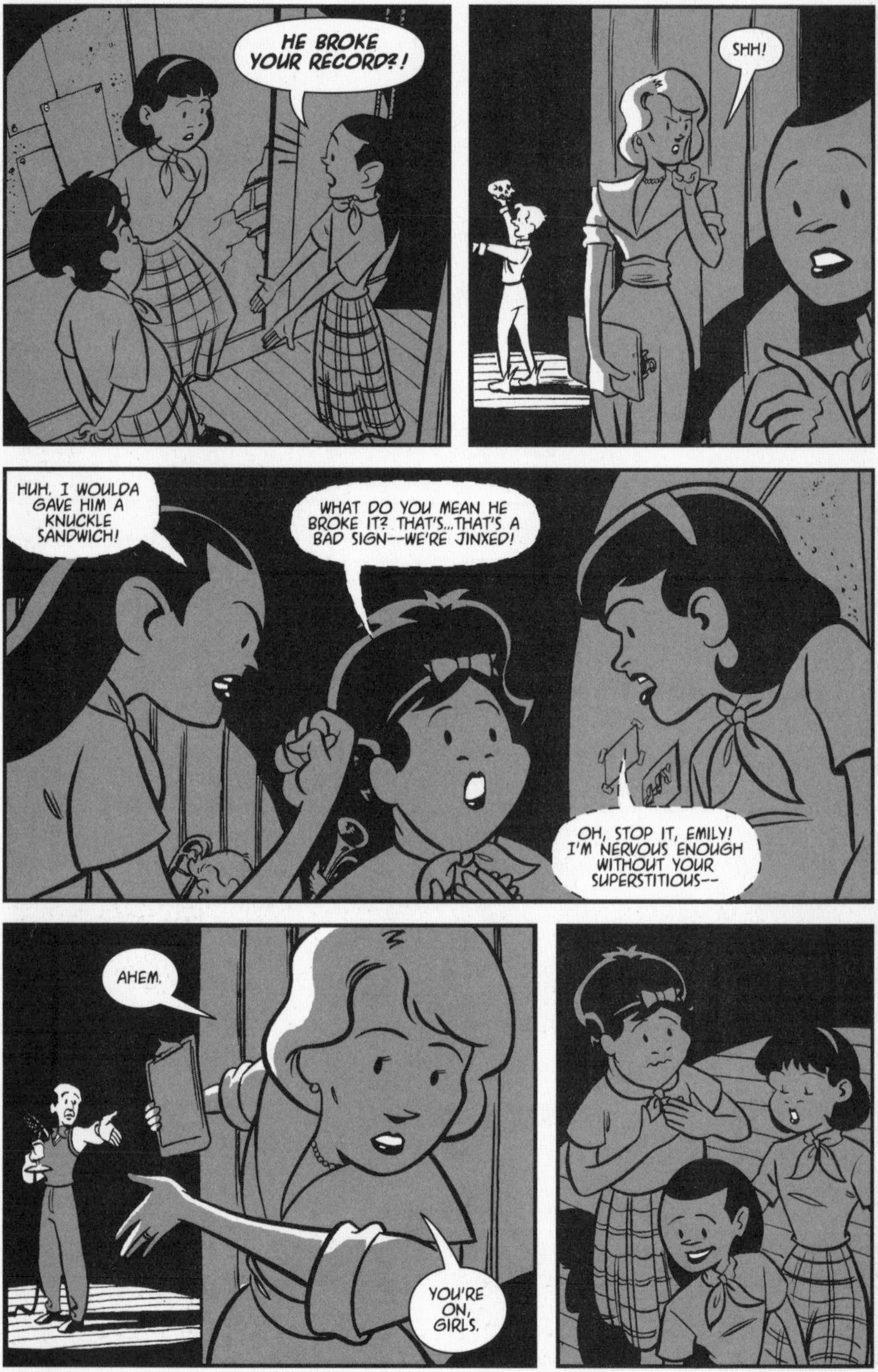
HE BROKE YOUR RECORD?!
SHH!
HUH. I WOULDA GAVE HIM A KNUCKLE SANDWICH!
WHAT DO YOU MEAN HE BROKE IT? THAT'S...THAT'S A BAD SIGN--WE'RE JINXED!
OH, STOP IT, EMILY! I'M NERVOUS ENOUGH WITHOUT YOUR SUPERSTITIOUS--
AHEM.
YOU'RE ON, GIRLS.

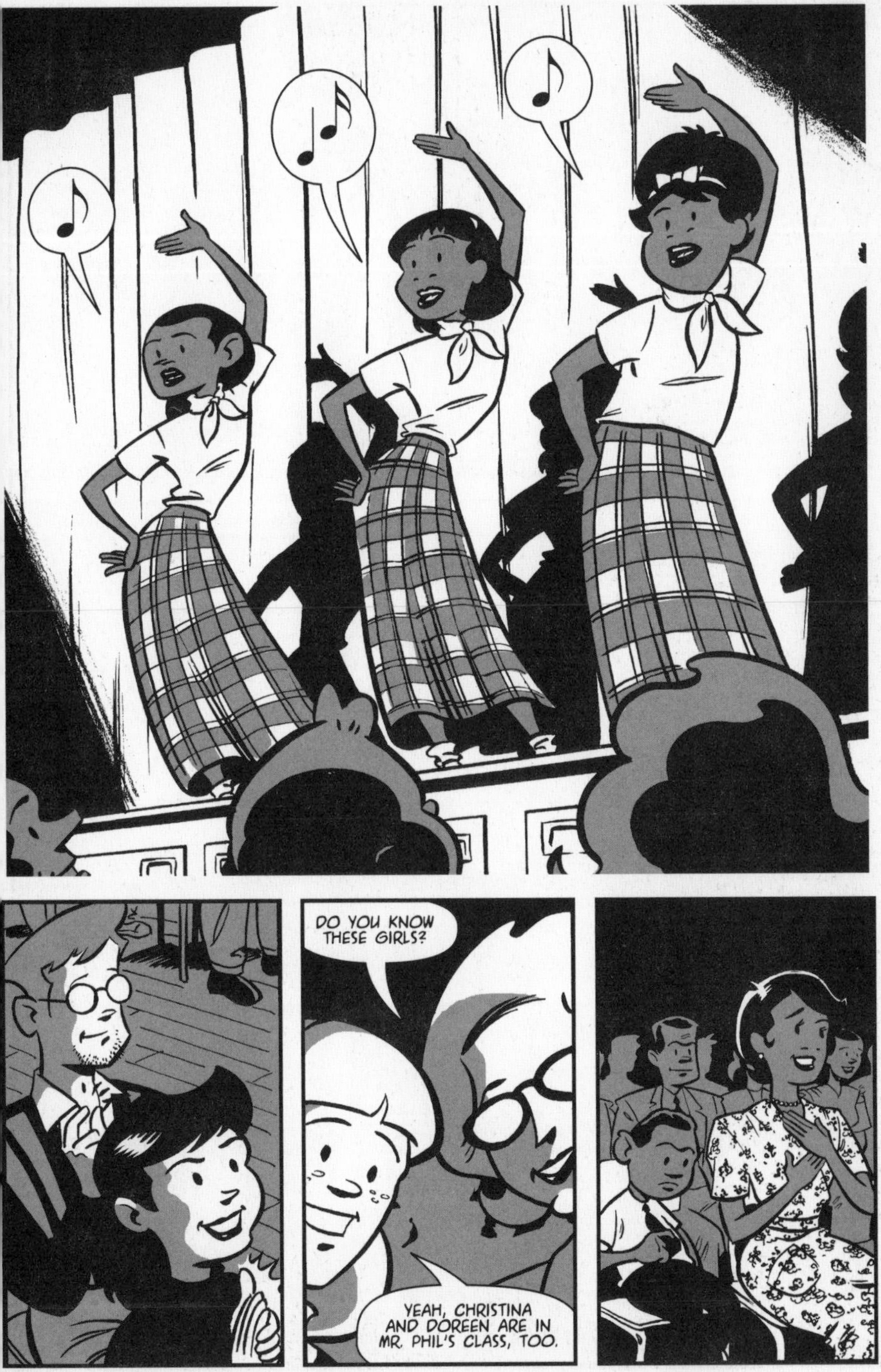
DO YOU KNOW THESE GIRLS?
YEAH, CHRISTINA AND DOREEN ARE IN MR. PHIL'S CLASS, TOO.

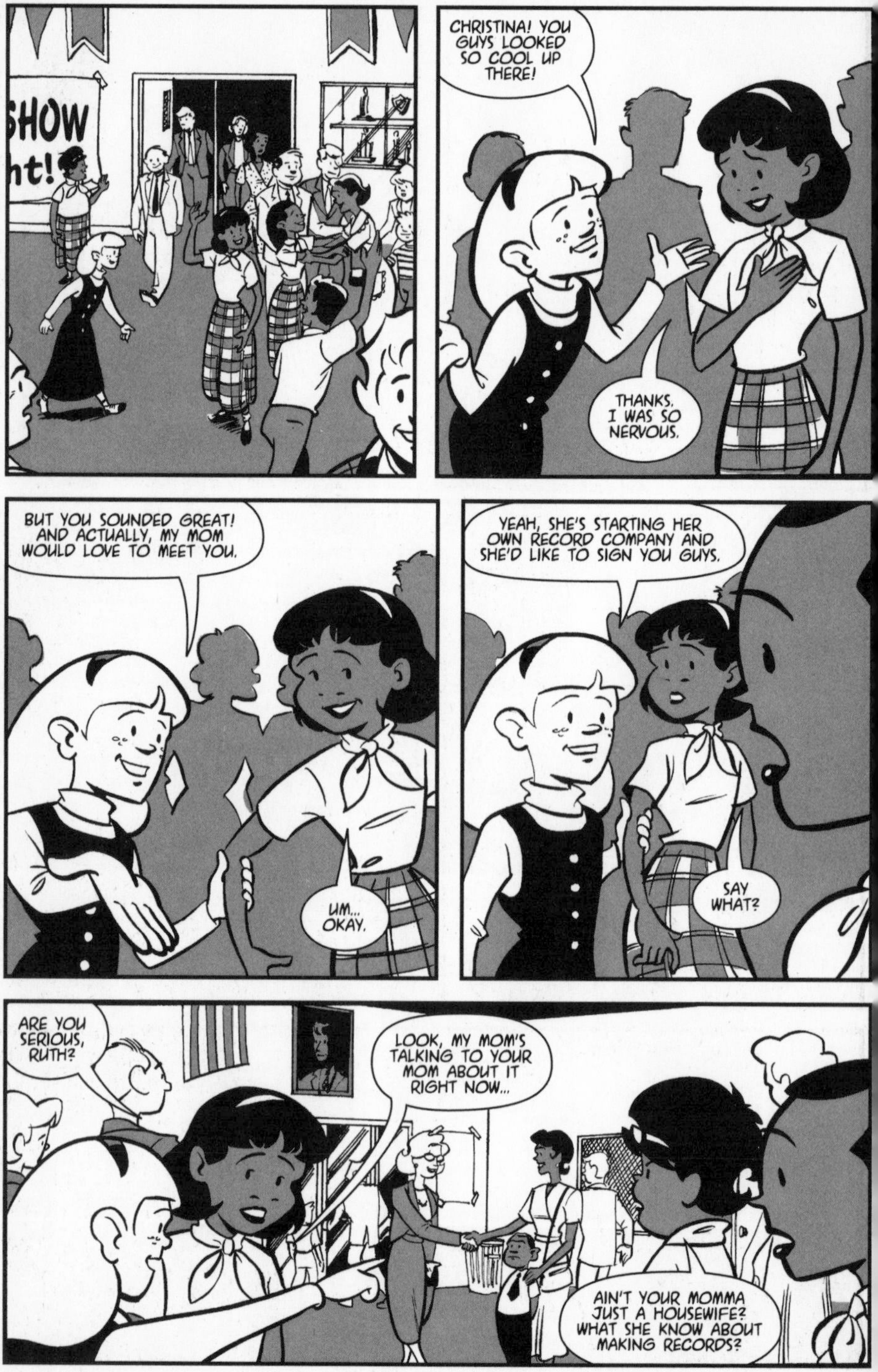
SHOW
ht!
CHRISTINA! YOU GUYS LOOKED SO COOL UP THERE!
THANKS. I WAS SO NERVOUS.
BUT YOU SOUNDED GREAT! AND ACTUALLY, MY MOM WOULD LOVE TO MEET YOU.
UM... OKAY.
YEAH, SHE'S STARTING HER OWN RECORD COMPANY AND SHE'D LIKE TO SIGN YOU GUYS.
SAY WHAT?
ARE YOU SERIOUS, RUTH?
LOOK, MY MOM'S TALKING TO YOUR MOM ABOUT IT RIGHT NOW...
AIN'T YOUR MOMMA JUST A HOUSEWIFE? WHAT SHE KNOW ABOUT MAKING RECORDS?

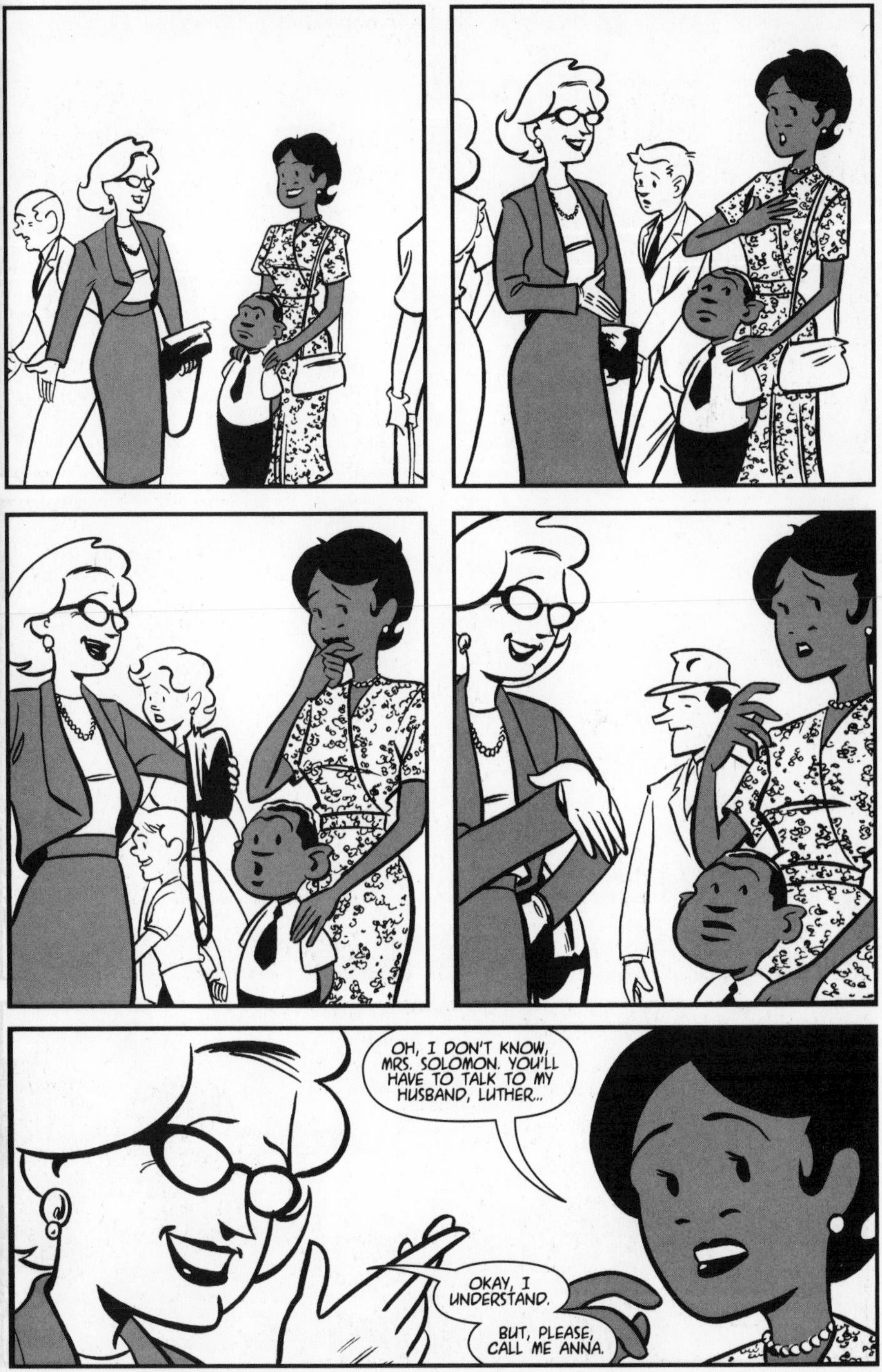
OH, I DON'T KNOW, MRS. SOLOMON. YOU'LL HAVE TO TALK TO MY HUSBAND, LUTHER...
OKAY, I UNDERSTAND.
BUT, PLEASE, CALL ME ANNA.

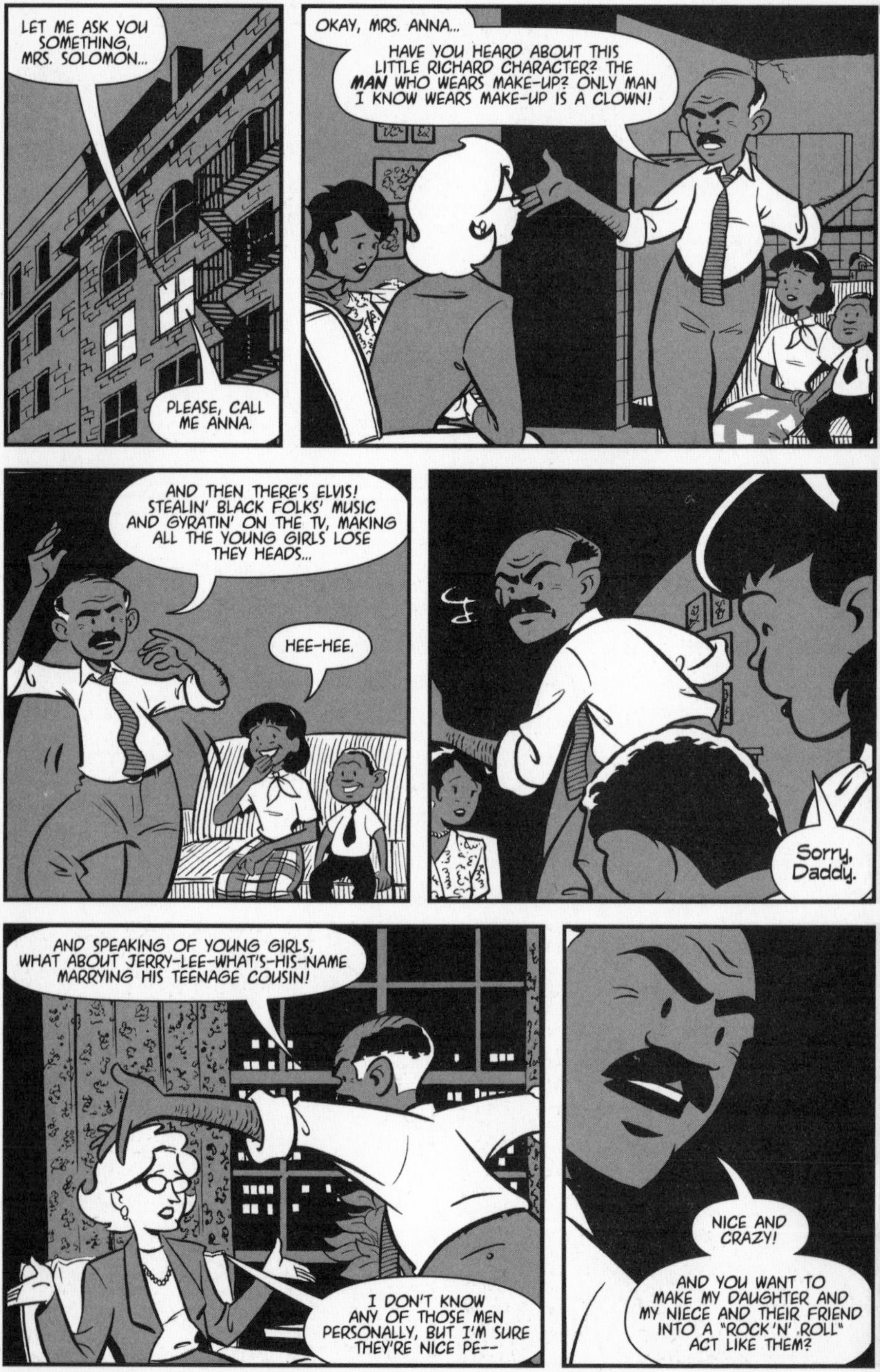
LET ME ASK YOU SOMETHING, MRS. SOLOMON...
PLEASE, CALL ME ANNA.
OKAY, MRS. ANNA...
HAVE YOU HEARD ABOUT THIS LITTLE RICHARD CHARACTER? THE MAN WHO WEARS MAKE-UP? ONLY MAN I KNOW WEARS MAKE-UP IS A CLOWN!
AND THEN THERE'S ELVIS! STEALIN' BLACK FOLKS' MUSIC AND GYRATIN' ON THE TV, MAKING ALL THE YOUNG GIRLS LOSE THEY HEADS...
HEE-HEE.
Sorry, Daddy.
AND SPEAKING OF YOUNG GIRLS, WHAT ABOUT JERRY-LEE-WHAT'S-HIS-NAME MARRYING HIS TEENAGE COUSIN!
I DON'T KNOW ANY OF THOSE MEN PERSONALLY, BUT I'M SURE THEY'RE NICE PE--
NICE AND CRAZY!
AND YOU WANT TO MAKE MY DAUGHTER AND MY NIECE AND THEIR FRIEND INTO A "ROCK 'N' ROLL" ACT LIKE THEM?

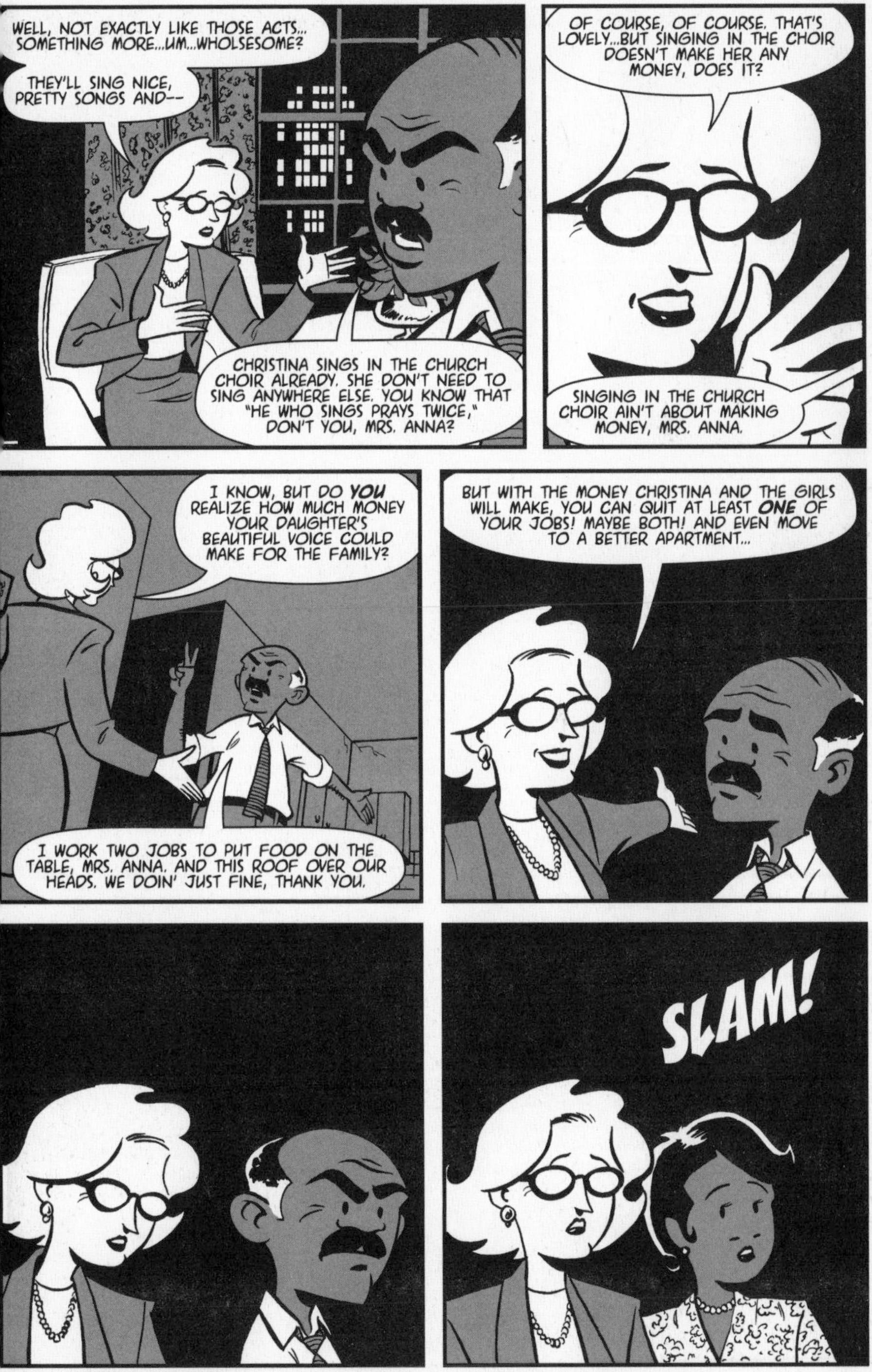
WELL, NOT EXACTLY LIKE THOSE ACTS... SOMETHING MORE...UM...WHOLSESOME?
THEY'LL SING NICE, PRETTY SONGS AND--
CHRISTINA SINGS IN THE CHURCH CHOIR ALREADY. SHE DON'T NEED TO SING ANYWHERE ELSE. YOU KNOW THAT "HE WHO SINGS PRAYS TWICE," DON'T YOU, MRS. ANNA?
OF COURSE, OF COURSE. THAT'S LOVELY...BUT SINGING IN THE CHOIR DOESN'T MAKE HER ANY MONEY, DOES IT?
SINGING IN THE CHURCH CHOIR AIN'T ABOUT MAKING MONEY, MRS. ANNA.
I KNOW, BUT DO YOU REALIZE HOW MUCH MONEY YOUR DAUGHTER'S BEAUTIFUL VOICE COULD MAKE FOR THE FAMILY?
I WORK TWO JOBS TO PUT FOOD ON THE TABLE, MRS. ANNA. AND THIS ROOF OVER OUR HEADS. WE DOIN' JUST FINE, THANK YOU.
BUT WITH THE MONEY CHRISTINA AND THE GIRLS WILL MAKE, YOU CAN QUIT AT LEAST ONE OF YOUR JOBS! MAYBE BOTH! AND EVEN MOVE TO A BETTER APARTMENT...
SLAM!

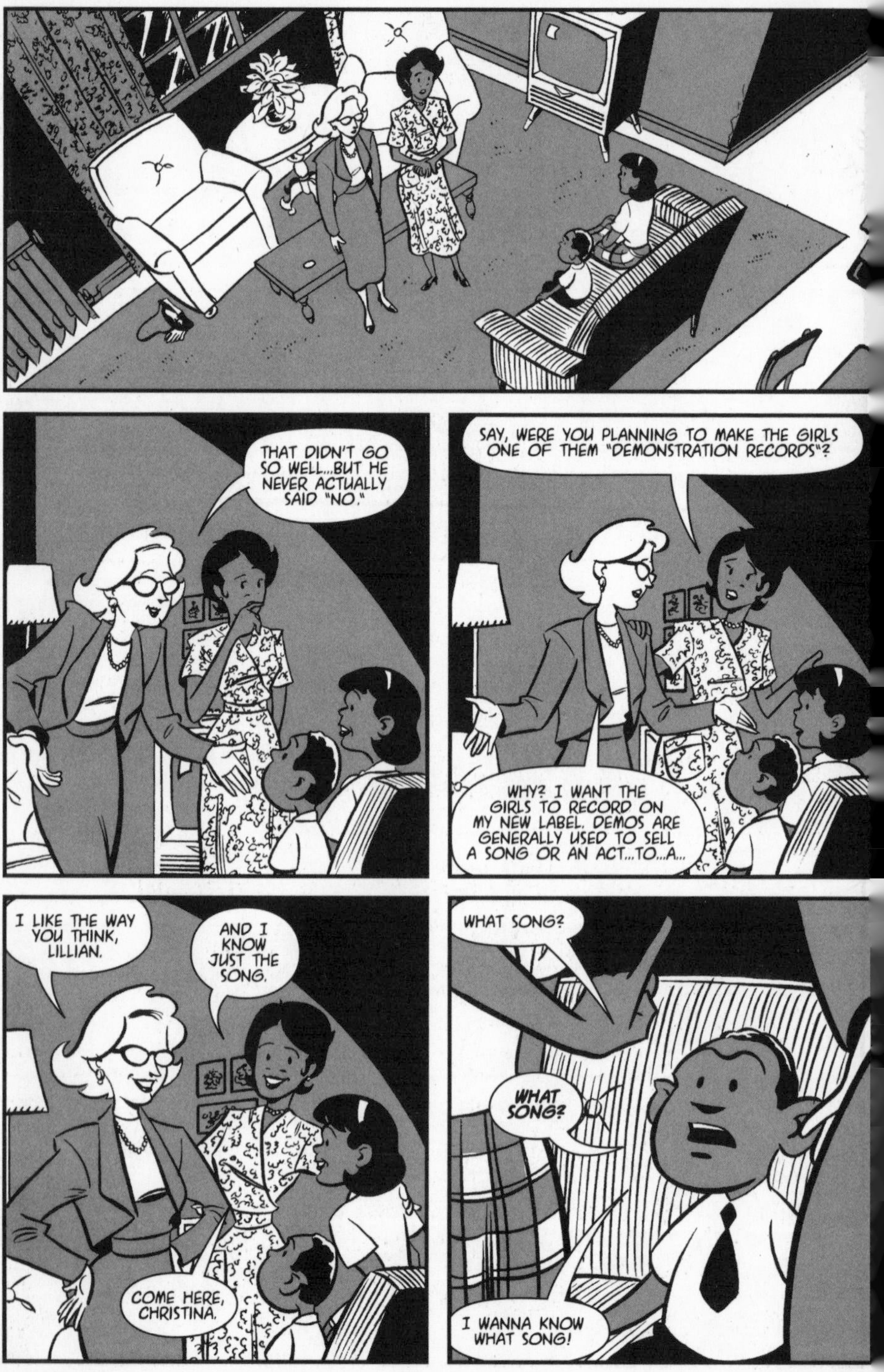
THAT DIDN'T GO SO WELL...BUT HE NEVER ACTUALLY SAID "NO."
SAY, WERE YOU PLANNING TO MAKE THE GIRLS ONE OF THEM "DEMONSTRATION RECORDS"?
WHY? I WANT THE GIRLS TO RECORD ON MY NEW LABEL. DEMOS ARE GENERALLY USED TO SELL A SONG OR AN ACT...TO...A...
I LIKE THE WAY YOU THINK, LILLIAN.
AND I KNOW JUST THE SONG.
COME HERE, CHRISTINA.
WHAT SONG?
WHAT SONG?
I WANNA KNOW WHAT SONG!

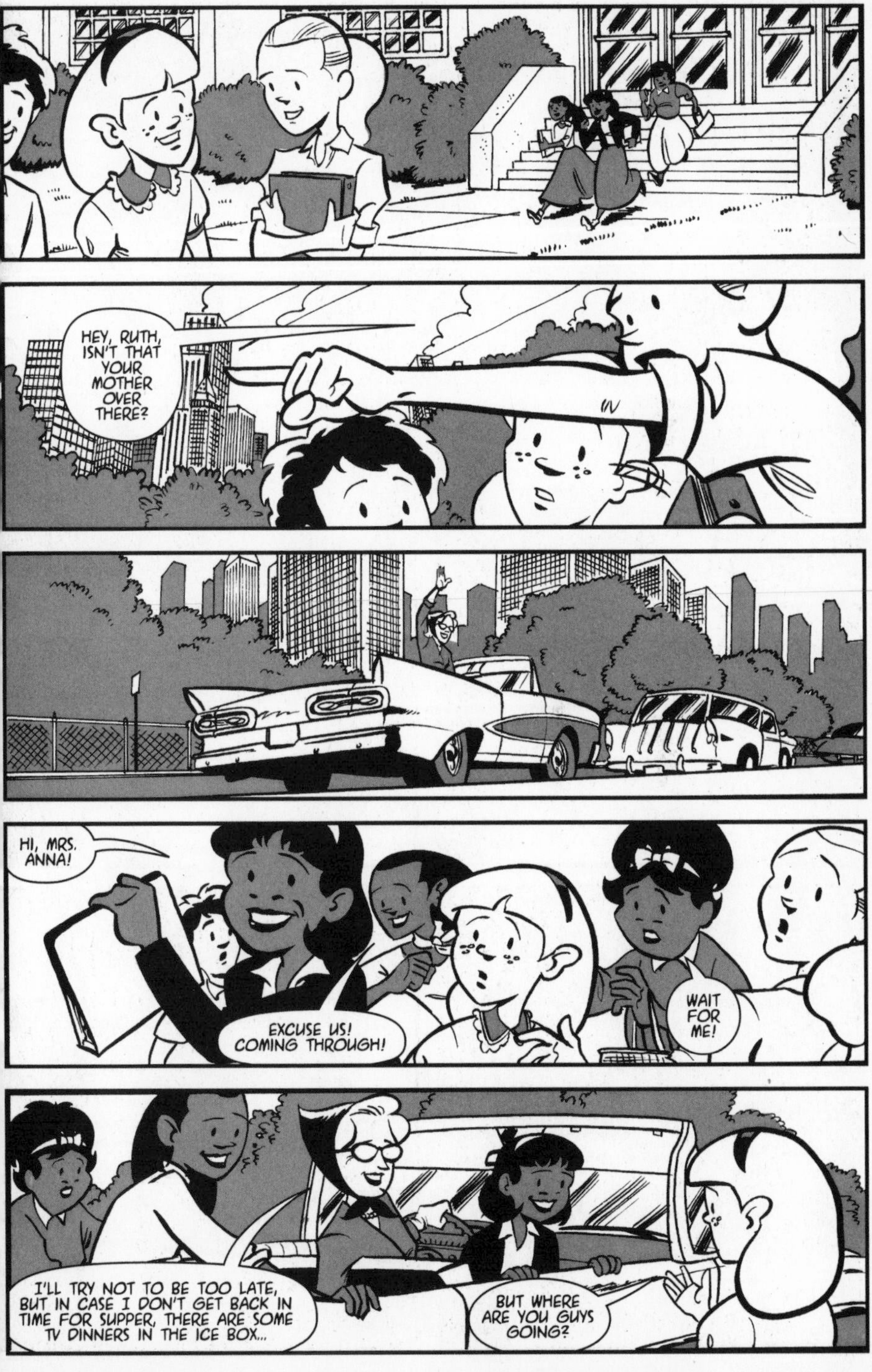
HEY, RUTH, ISN'T THAT YOUR MOTHER OVER THERE?
HI, MRS. ANNA!
EXCUSE US! COMING THROUGH!
WAIT FOR ME!
I'LL TRY NOT TO BE TOO LATE, BUT IN CASE I DON'T GET BACK IN TIME FOR SUPPER, THERE ARE SOME TV DINNERS IN THE ICE BOX...
BUT WHERE ARE YOU GUYS GOING?

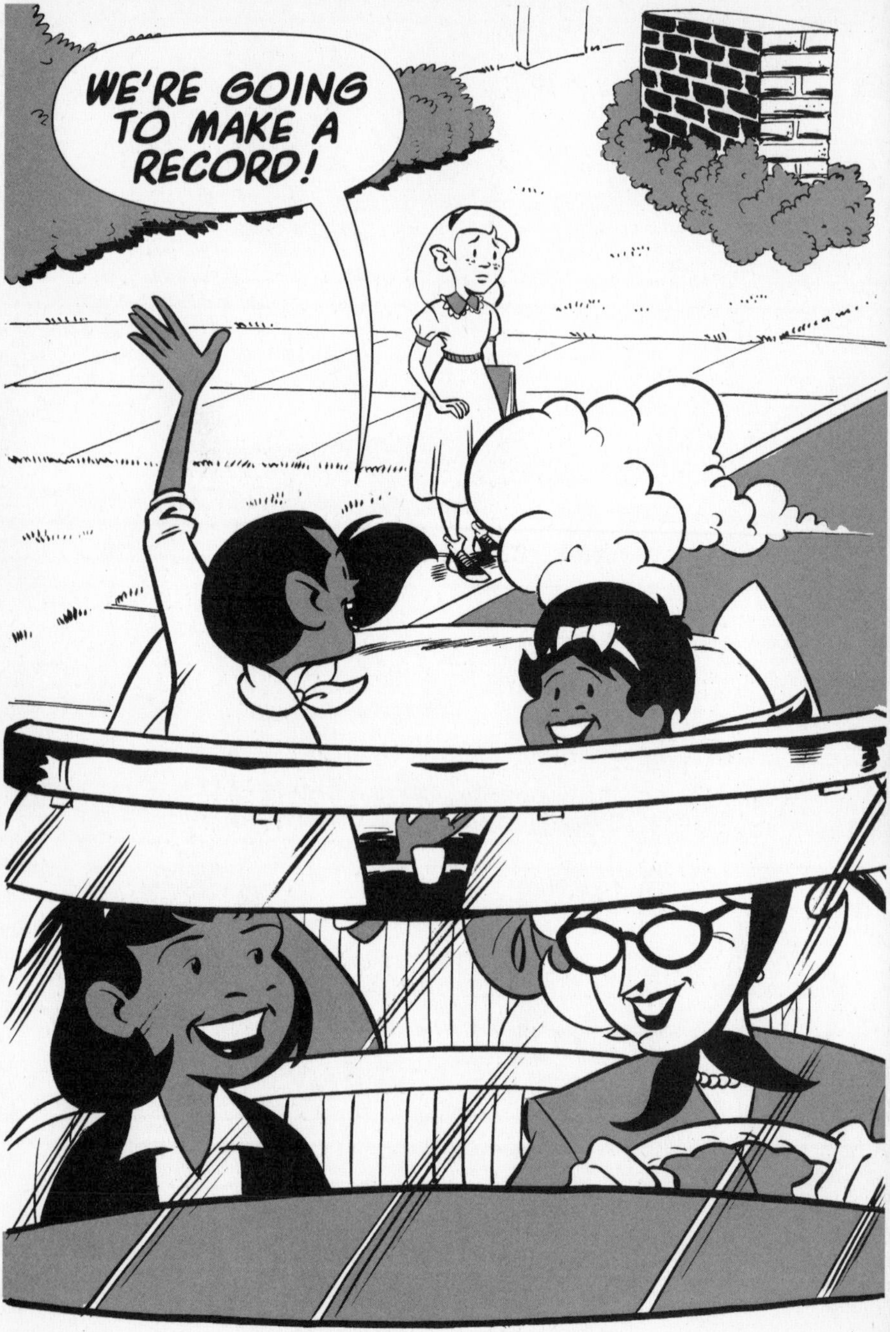
WE'RE GOING TO MAKE A RECORD!

CHAPTER 2
"Dedicated to the One I Love"

"Harmony Plaza recording studio. Making a demonstration record."

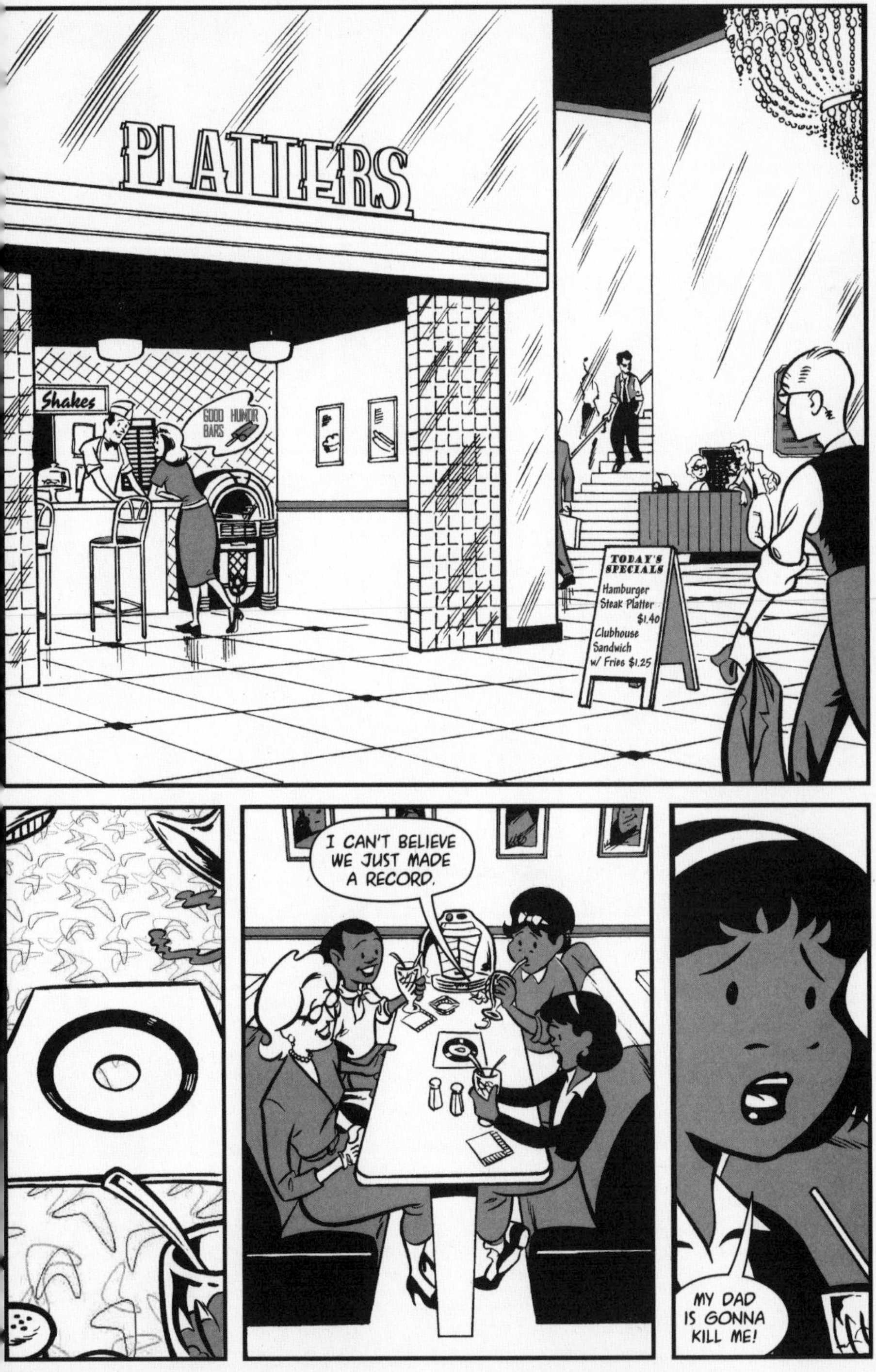
PLATTERS
Shakes
GOOD HUMOR BARS
TODAY'S SPECIALS
Hamburger Steak Platter $1.40
Clubhouse Sandwich w/ Fries $1.25
I CAN'T BELIEVE WE JUST MADE A RECORD.
MY DAD IS GONNA KILL ME!

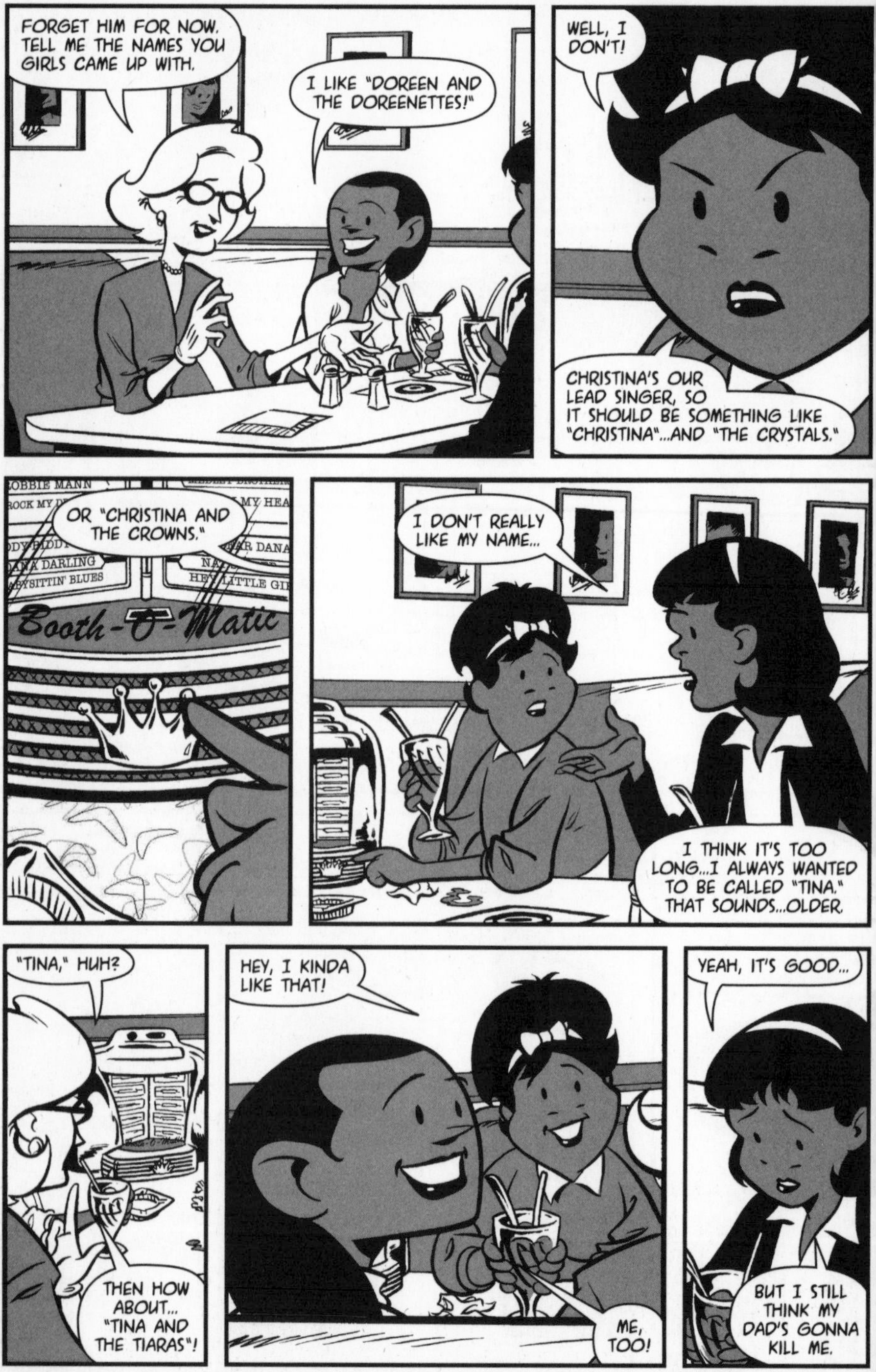
FORGET HIM FOR NOW. TELL ME THE NAMES YOU GIRLS CAME UP WITH.
I LIKE "DOREEN AND THE DOREENETTES!"
WELL, I DON'T!
CHRISTINA'S OUR LEAD SINGER, SO IT SHOULD BE SOMETHING LIKE "CHRISTINA"...AND "THE CRYSTALS."
OR "CHRISTINA AND THE CROWNS."
Booth-O-Matic
I DON'T REALLY LIKE MY NAME...
I THINK IT'S TOO LONG...I ALWAYS WANTED TO BE CALLED "TINA." THAT SOUNDS...OLDER.
"TINA," HUH?
THEN HOW ABOUT... "TINA AND THE TIARAS"!
HEY, I KINDA LIKE THAT!
ME, TOO!
YEAH, IT'S GOOD...
BUT I STILL THINK MY DAD'S GONNA KILL ME.

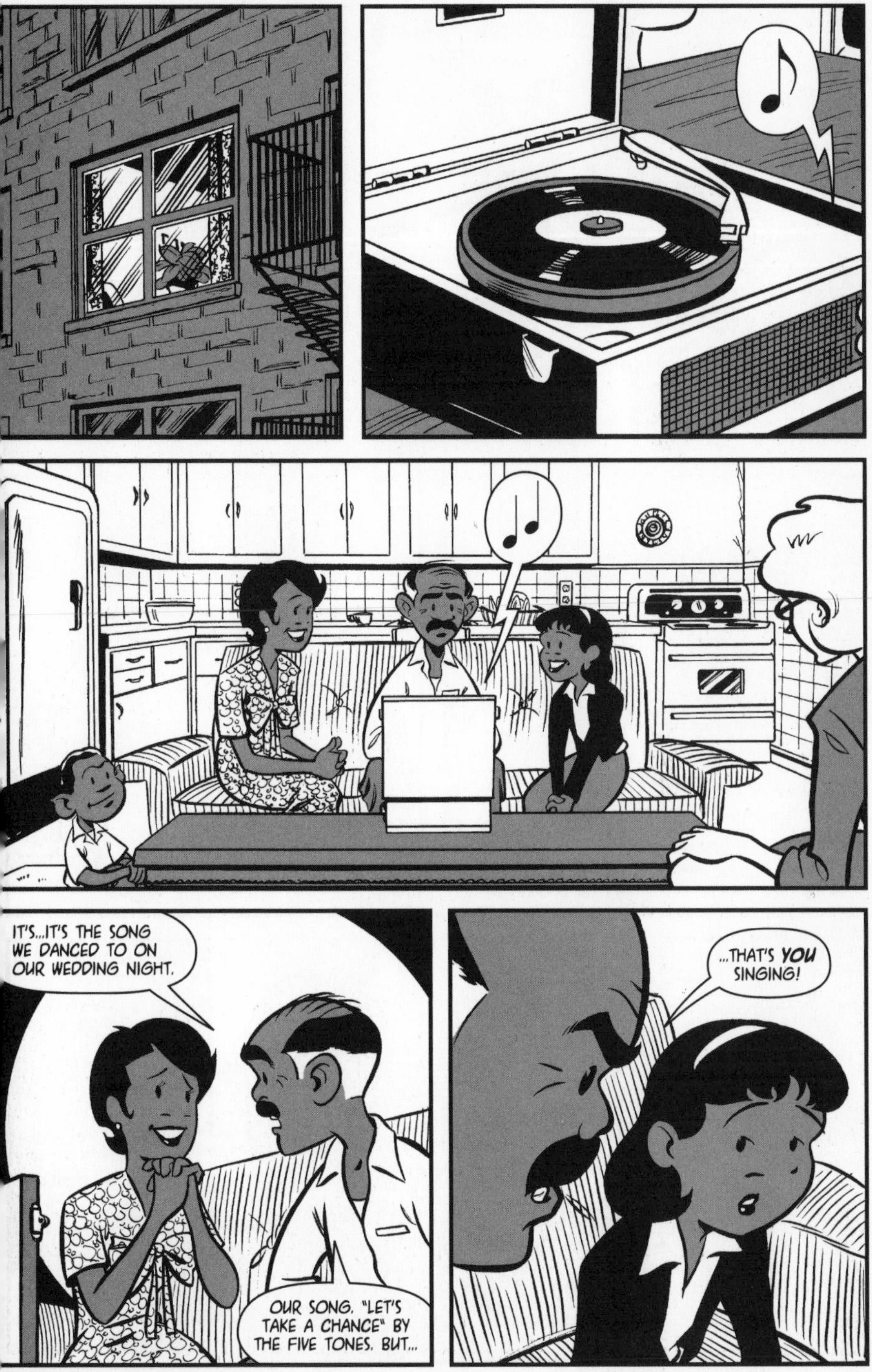
IT'S...IT'S THE SONG WE DANCED TO ON OUR WEDDING NIGHT.
OUR SONG. "LET'S TAKE A CHANCE" BY THE FIVE TONES. BUT...
...THAT'S *YOU* SINGING!

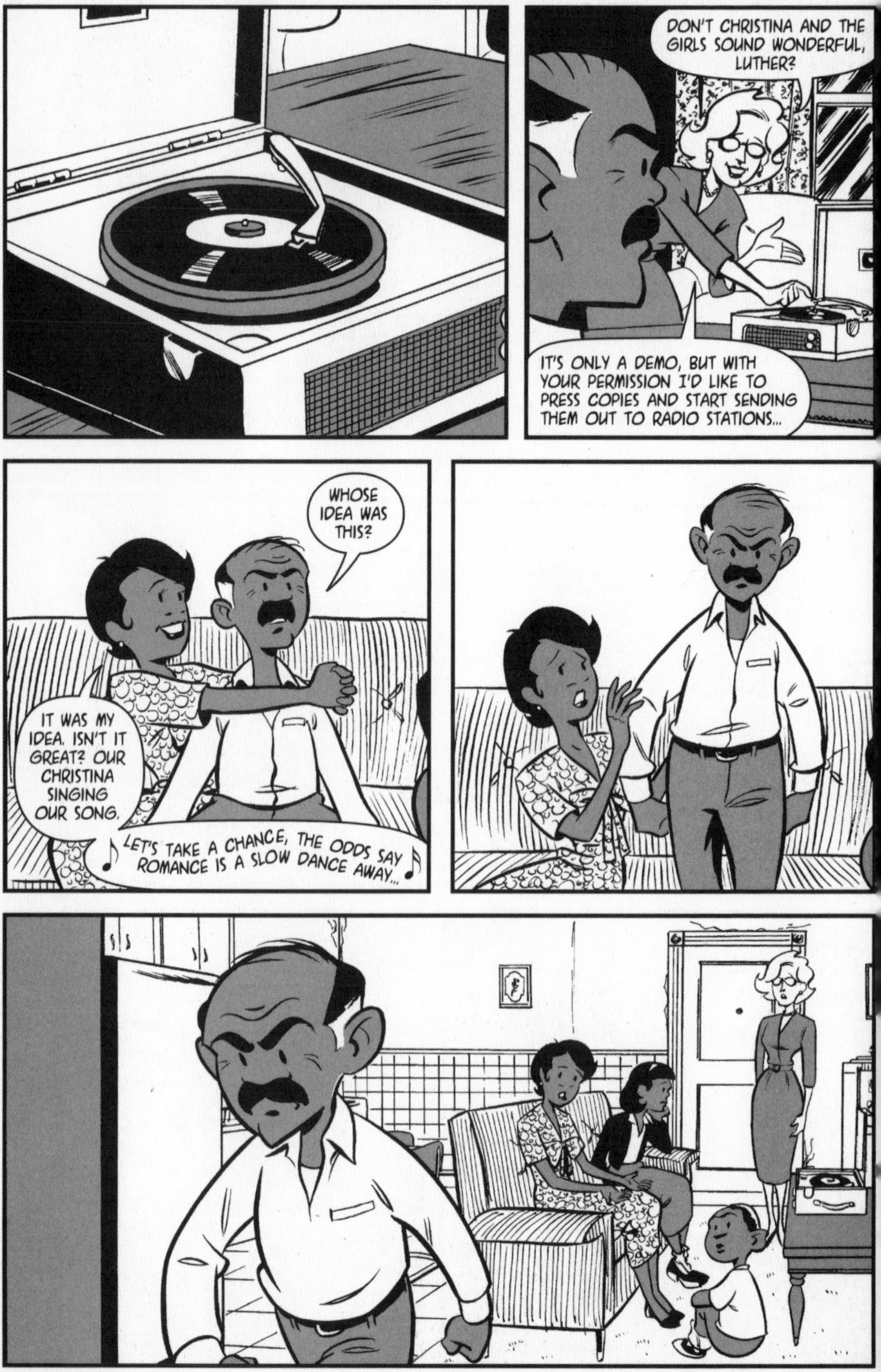
DON'T CHRISTINA AND THE GIRLS SOUND WONDERFUL, LUTHER?
IT'S ONLY A DEMO, BUT WITH YOUR PERMISSION I'D LIKE TO PRESS COPIES AND START SENDING THEM OUT TO RADIO STATIONS...
WHOSE IDEA WAS THIS?
IT WAS MY IDEA. ISN'T IT GREAT? OUR CHRISTINA SINGING OUR SONG.
♪ LET'S TAKE A CHANCE, THE ODDS SAY ROMANCE IS A SLOW DANCE AWAY... ♪

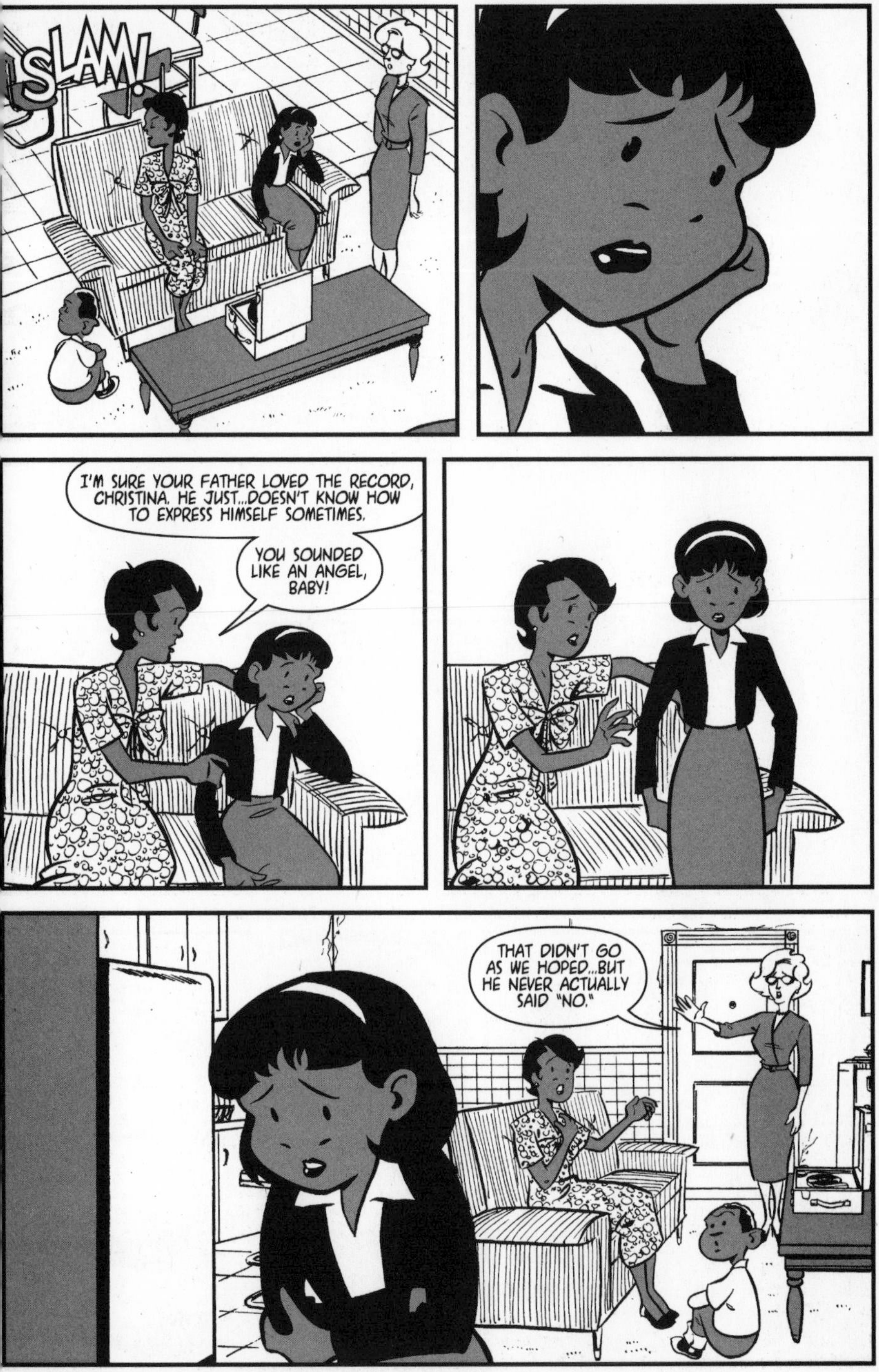
SLAM!
I'M SURE YOUR FATHER LOVED THE RECORD, CHRISTINA. HE JUST...DOESN'T KNOW HOW TO EXPRESS HIMSELF SOMETIMES.
YOU SOUNDED LIKE AN ANGEL, BABY!
THAT DIDN'T GO AS WE HOPED...BUT HE NEVER ACTUALLY SAID "NO."

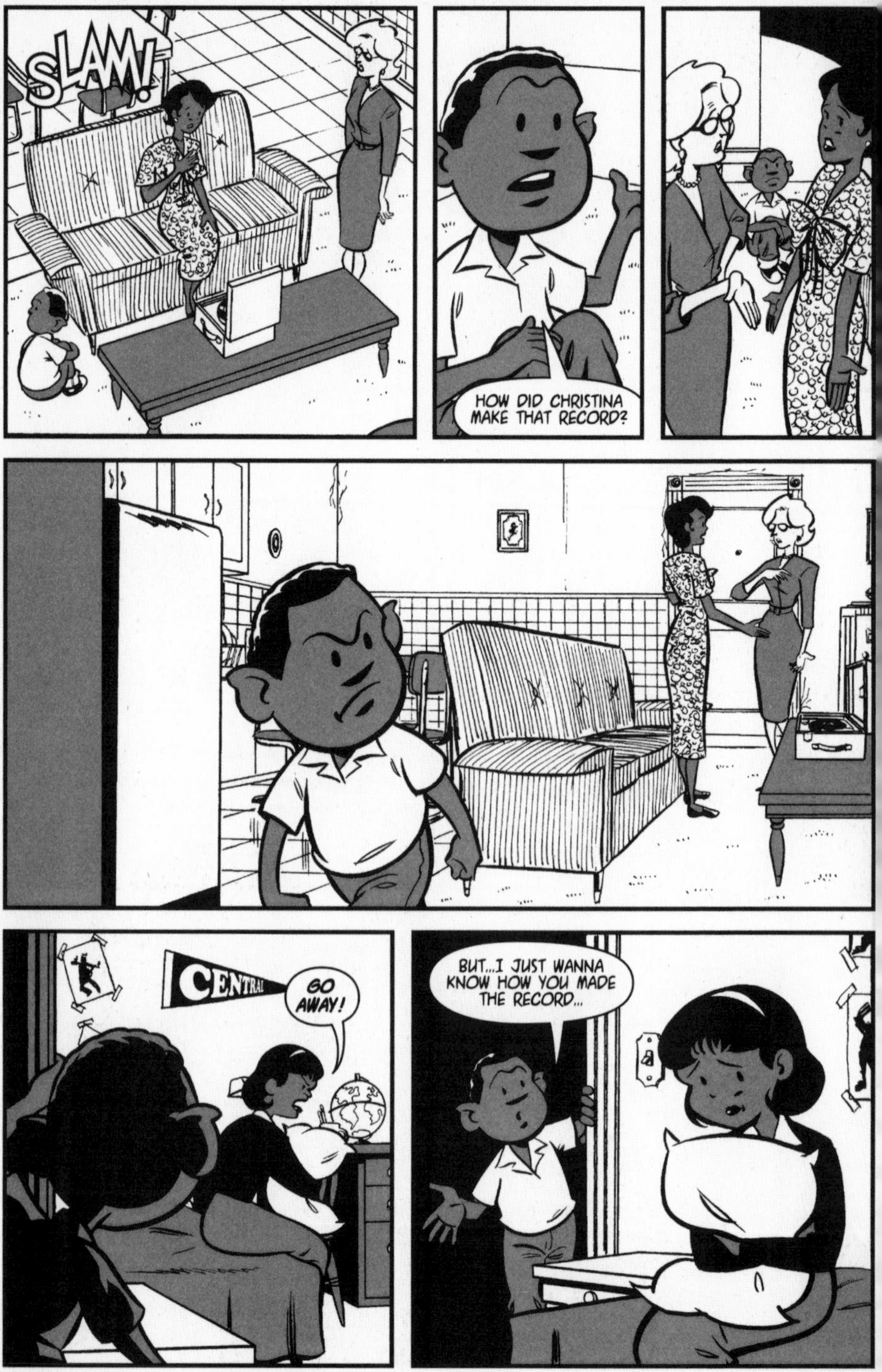
SLAM!
HOW DID CHRISTINA MAKE THAT RECORD?
CENTRAL
GO AWAY!
BUT...I JUST WANNA KNOW HOW YOU MADE THE RECORD...

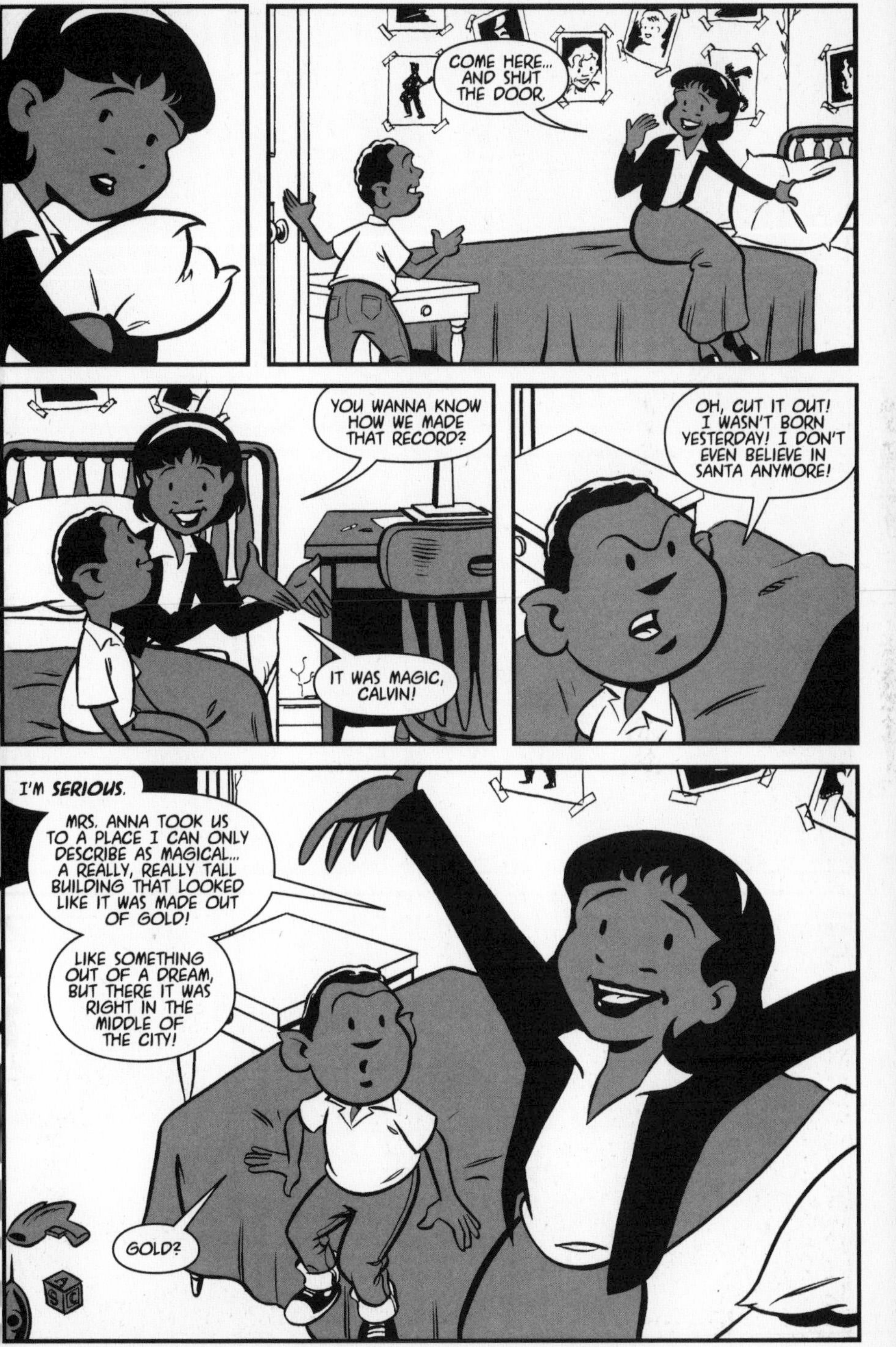
COME HERE... AND SHUT THE DOOR.
YOU WANNA KNOW HOW WE MADE THAT RECORD?
IT WAS MAGIC, CALVIN!
OH, CUT IT OUT! I WASN'T BORN YESTERDAY! I DON'T EVEN BELIEVE IN SANTA ANYMORE!
I'M **SERIOUS**.
MRS. ANNA TOOK US TO A PLACE I CAN ONLY DESCRIBE AS MAGICAL... A REALLY, REALLY TALL BUILDING THAT LOOKED LIKE IT WAS MADE OUT OF GOLD!
LIKE SOMETHING OUT OF A DREAM, BUT THERE IT WAS RIGHT IN THE MIDDLE OF THE CITY!
GOLD?

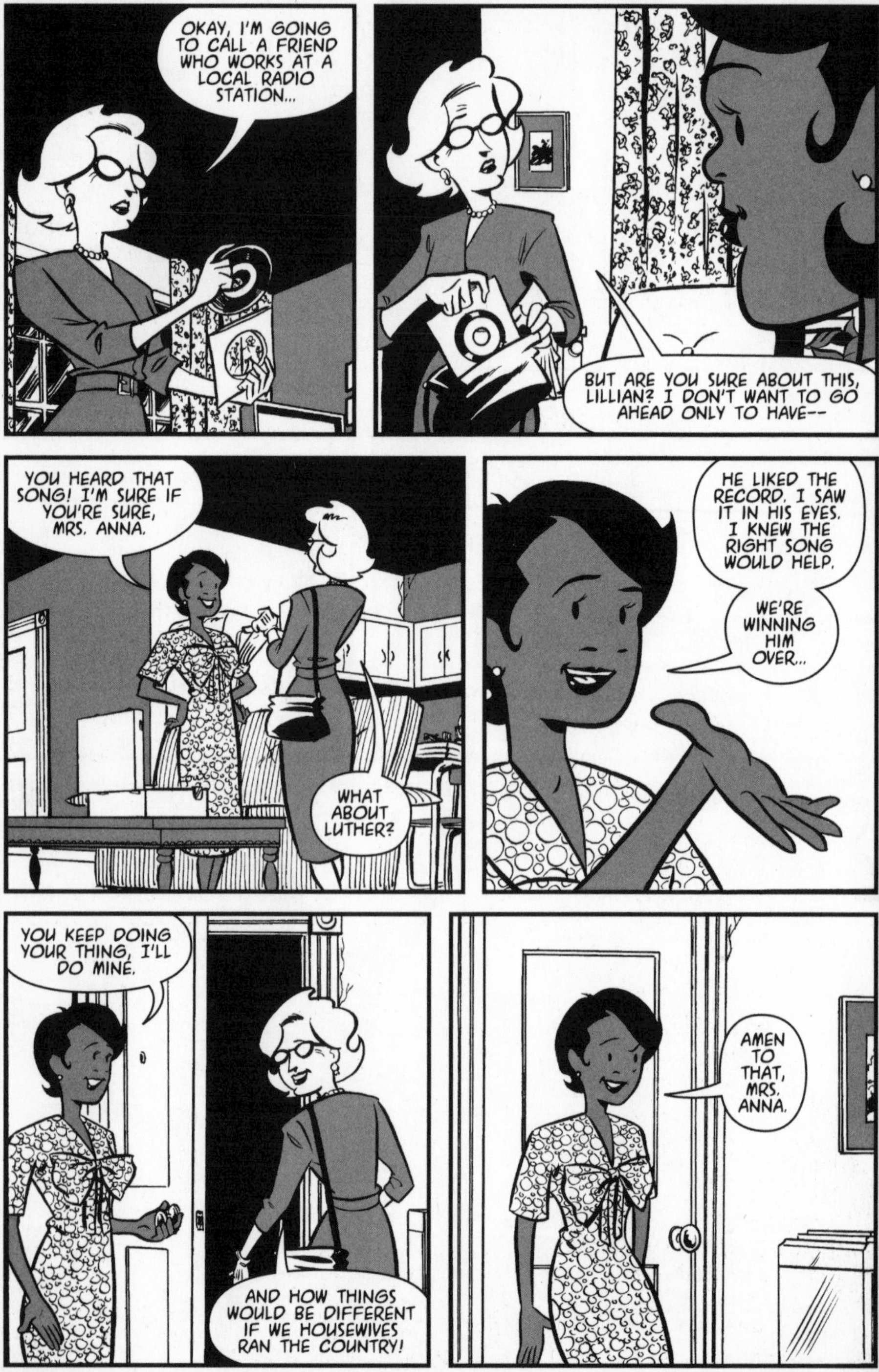
OKAY, I'M GOING TO CALL A FRIEND WHO WORKS AT A LOCAL RADIO STATION...
BUT ARE YOU SURE ABOUT THIS, LILLIAN? I DON'T WANT TO GO AHEAD ONLY TO HAVE--
YOU HEARD THAT SONG! I'M SURE IF YOU'RE SURE, MRS. ANNA.
WHAT ABOUT LUTHER?
HE LIKED THE RECORD. I SAW IT IN HIS EYES. I KNEW THE RIGHT SONG WOULD HELP.
WE'RE WINNING HIM OVER...
YOU KEEP DOING YOUR THING, I'LL DO MINE.
AND HOW THINGS WOULD BE DIFFERENT IF WE HOUSEWIVES RAN THE COUNTRY!
AMEN TO THAT, MRS. ANNA.

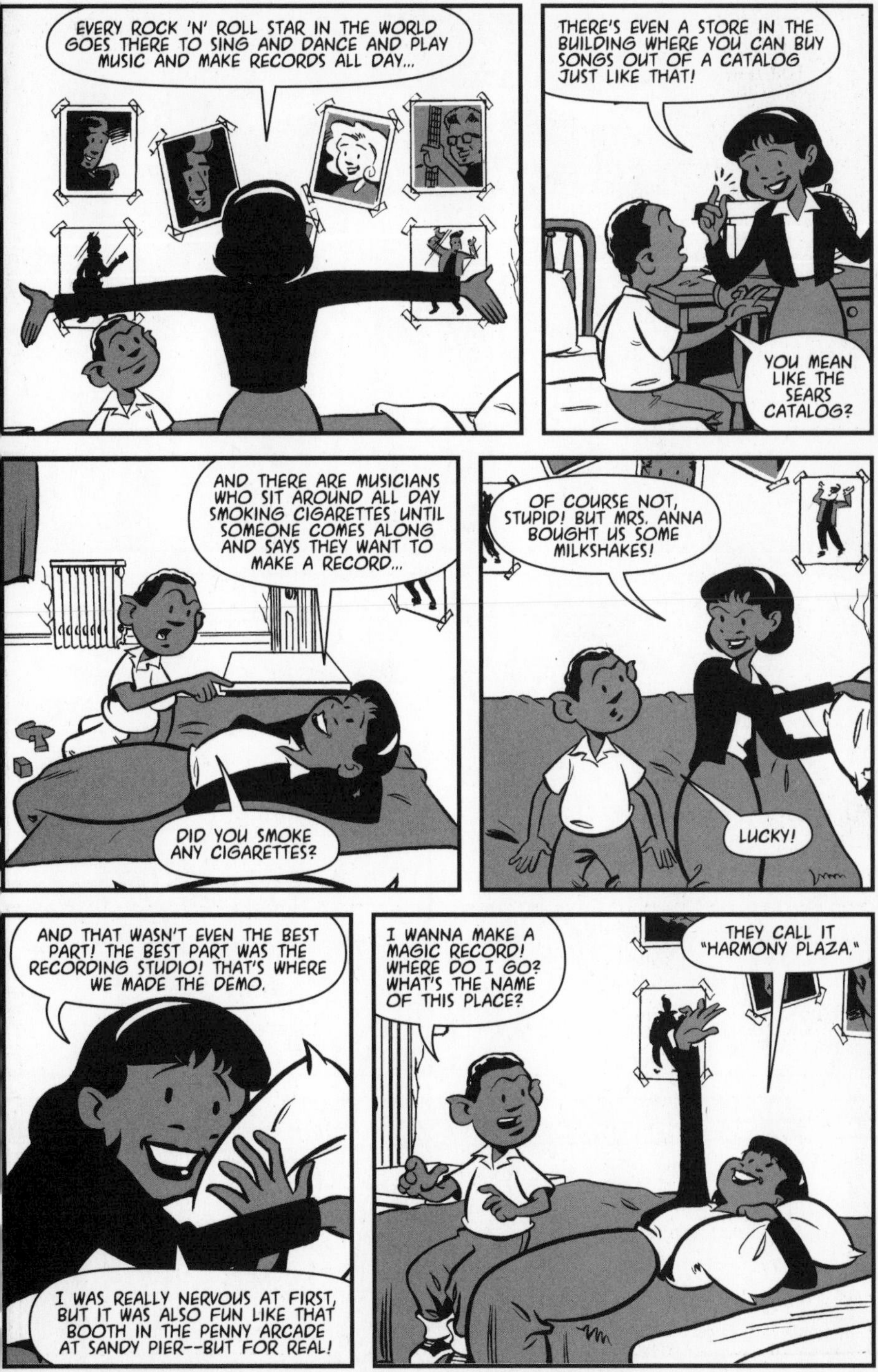
EVERY ROCK 'N' ROLL STAR IN THE WORLD GOES THERE TO SING AND DANCE AND PLAY MUSIC AND MAKE RECORDS ALL DAY...
THERE'S EVEN A STORE IN THE BUILDING WHERE YOU CAN BUY SONGS OUT OF A CATALOG JUST LIKE THAT!
YOU MEAN LIKE THE SEARS CATALOG?
AND THERE ARE MUSICIANS WHO SIT AROUND ALL DAY SMOKING CIGARETTES UNTIL SOMEONE COMES ALONG AND SAYS THEY WANT TO MAKE A RECORD...
DID YOU SMOKE ANY CIGARETTES?
OF COURSE NOT, STUPID! BUT MRS. ANNA BOUGHT US SOME MILKSHAKES!
LUCKY!
AND THAT WASN'T EVEN THE BEST PART! THE BEST PART WAS THE RECORDING STUDIO! THAT'S WHERE WE MADE THE DEMO.
I WAS REALLY NERVOUS AT FIRST, BUT IT WAS ALSO FUN LIKE THAT BOOTH IN THE PENNY ARCADE AT SANDY PIER--BUT FOR REAL!
I WANNA MAKE A MAGIC RECORD! WHERE DO I GO? WHAT'S THE NAME OF THIS PLACE?
THEY CALL IT "HARMONY PLAZA."

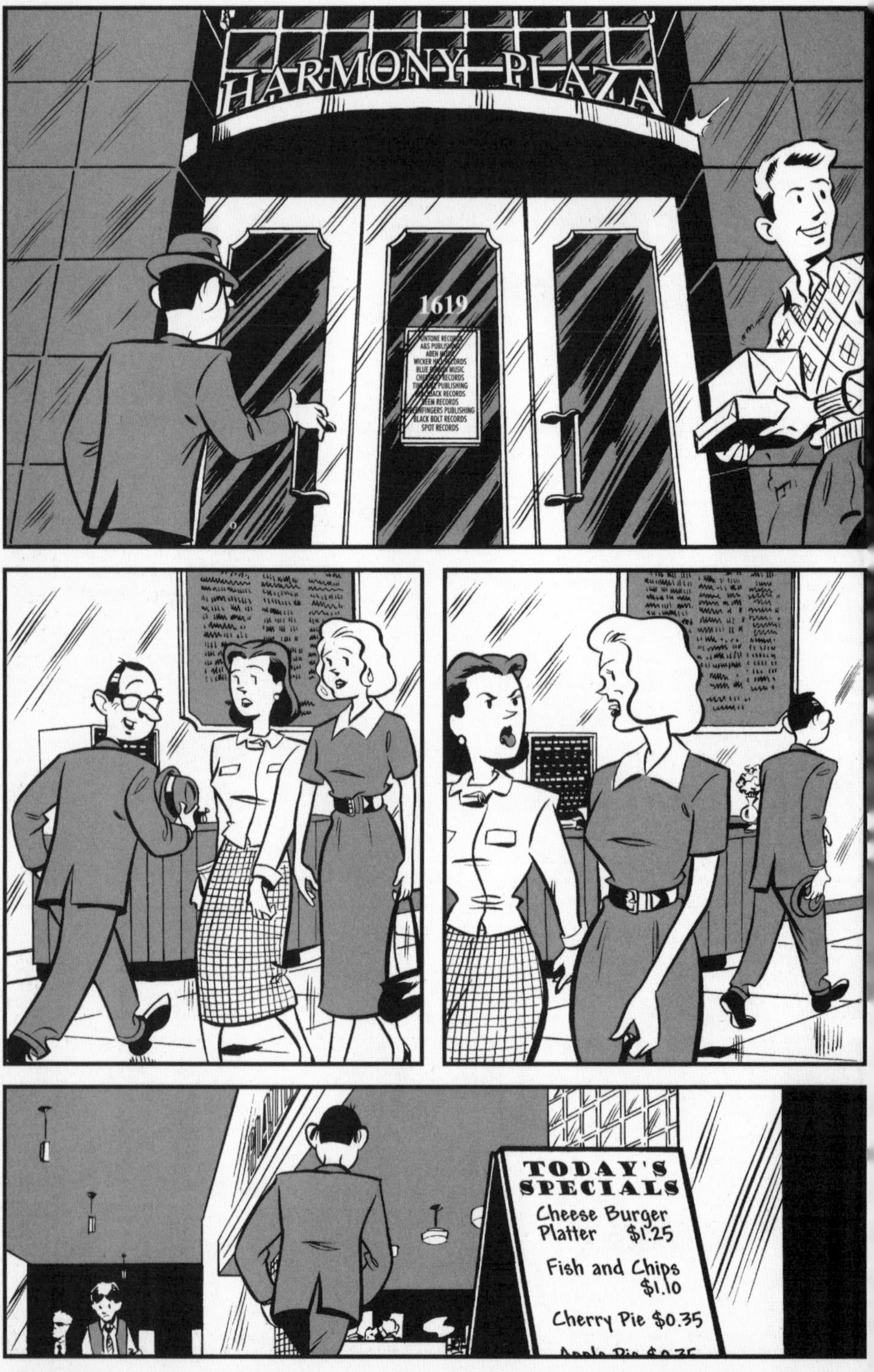
HARMONY PLAZA
1619
BLACK BOLT RECORDS
SPOT RECORDS
TODAY'S SPECIALS
Cheese Burger Platter $1.25
Fish and Chips $1.10
Cherry Pie $0.35

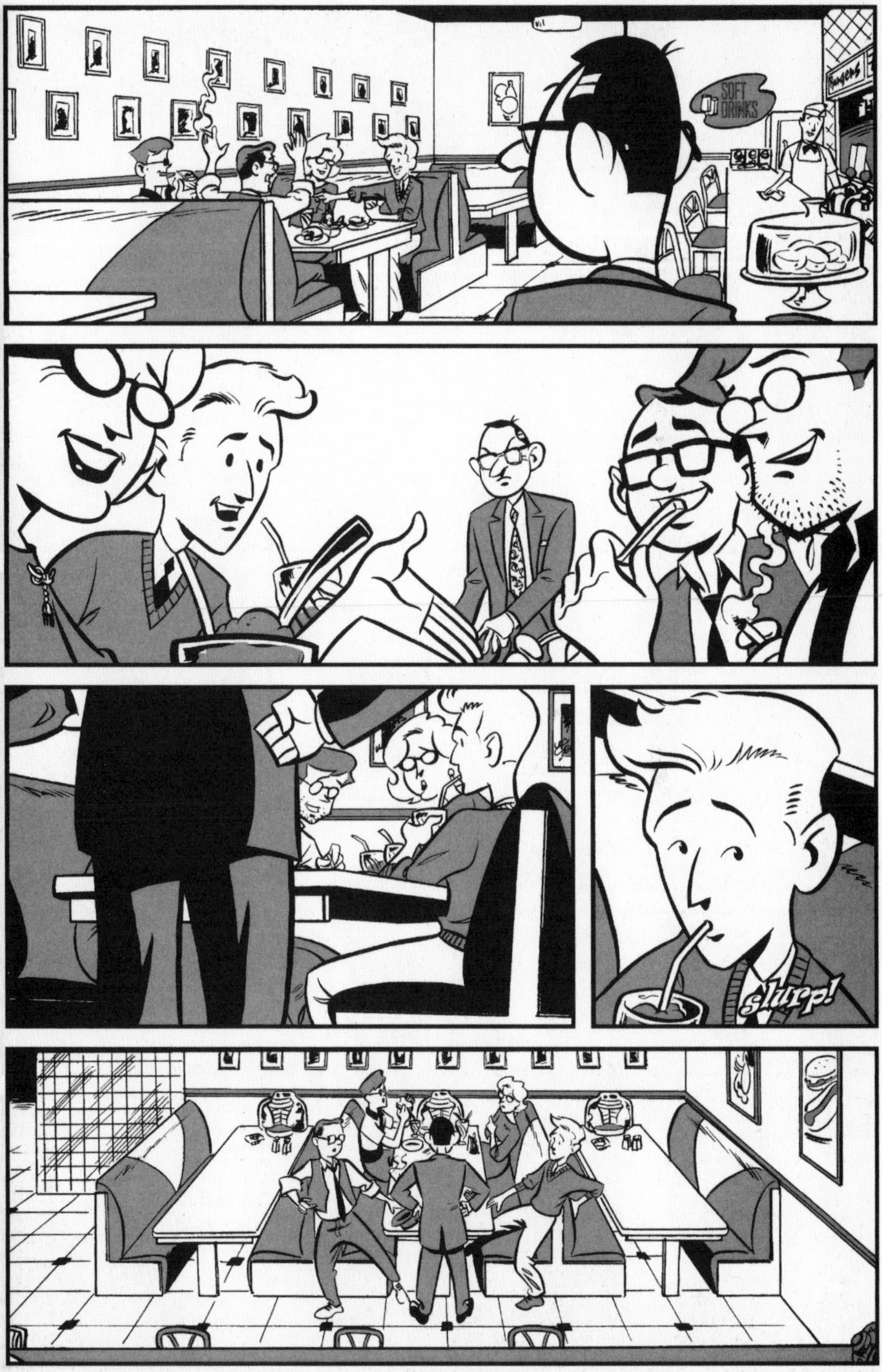
SOFT DRINKS
Burgers
slurp!

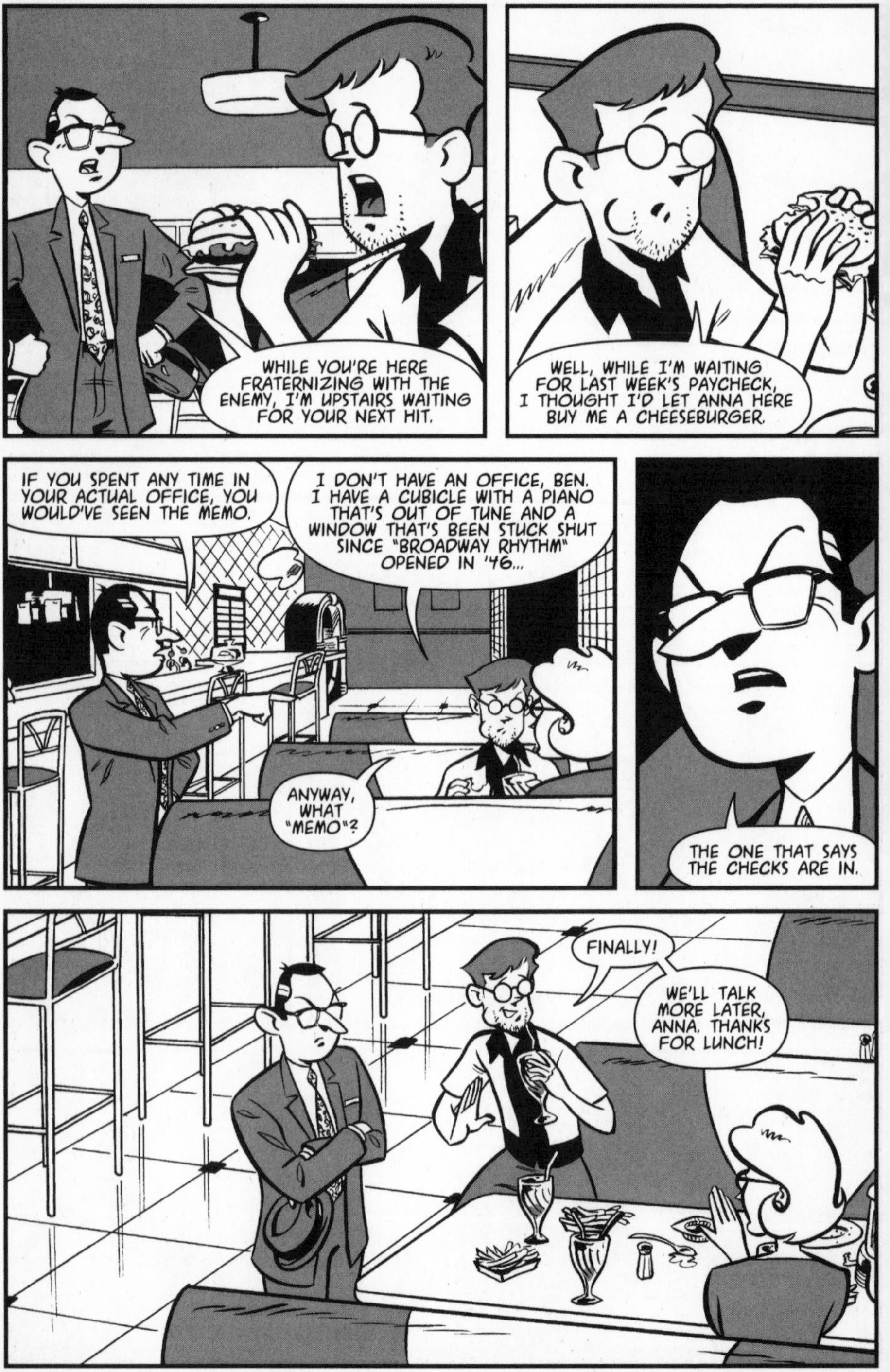
WHILE YOU'RE HERE FRATERNIZING WITH THE ENEMY, I'M UPSTAIRS WAITING FOR YOUR NEXT HIT.
WELL, WHILE I'M WAITING FOR LAST WEEK'S PAYCHECK, I THOUGHT I'D LET ANNA HERE BUY ME A CHEESEBURGER.
IF YOU SPENT ANY TIME IN YOUR ACTUAL OFFICE, YOU WOULD'VE SEEN THE MEMO.
I DON'T HAVE AN OFFICE, BEN. I HAVE A CUBICLE WITH A PIANO THAT'S OUT OF TUNE AND A WINDOW THAT'S BEEN STUCK SHUT SINCE "BROADWAY RHYTHM" OPENED IN '46...
ANYWAY, WHAT "MEMO"?
THE ONE THAT SAYS THE CHECKS ARE IN.
FINALLY!
WE'LL TALK MORE LATER, ANNA. THANKS FOR LUNCH!

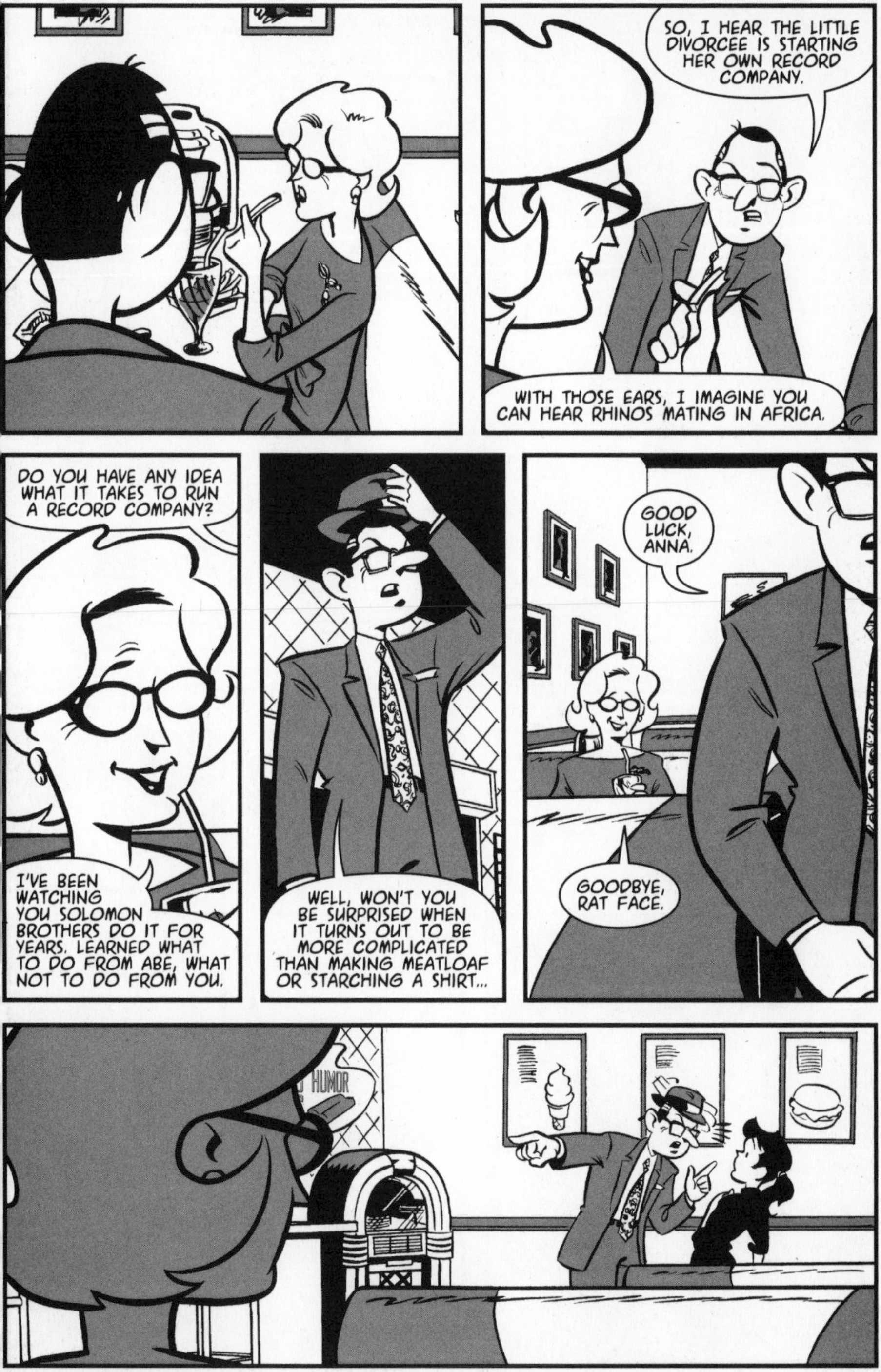
SO, I HEAR THE LITTLE DIVORCEE IS STARTING HER OWN RECORD COMPANY.
WITH THOSE EARS, I IMAGINE YOU CAN HEAR RHINOS MATING IN AFRICA.
DO YOU HAVE ANY IDEA WHAT IT TAKES TO RUN A RECORD COMPANY?
I'VE BEEN WATCHING YOU SOLOMON BROTHERS DO IT FOR YEARS. LEARNED WHAT TO DO FROM ABE, WHAT NOT TO DO FROM YOU.
WELL, WON'T YOU BE SURPRISED WHEN IT TURNS OUT TO BE MORE COMPLICATED THAN MAKING MEATLOAF OR STARCHING A SHIRT...
GOOD LUCK, ANNA.
GOODBYE, RAT FACE.
HUMOR

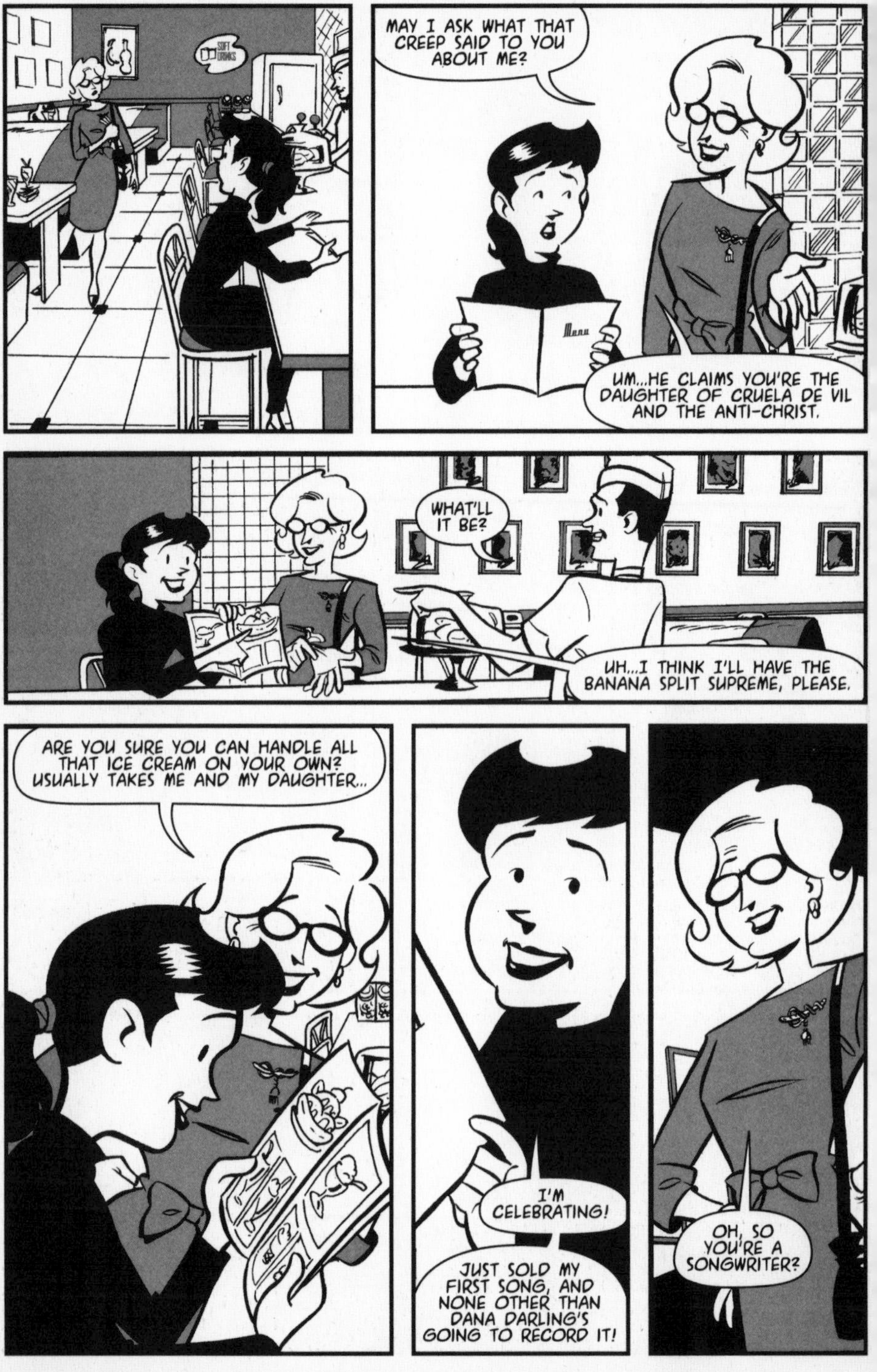
SOFT DRINKS
MAY I ASK WHAT THAT CREEP SAID TO YOU ABOUT ME?
Menu
UM...HE CLAIMS YOU'RE THE DAUGHTER OF CRUELA DE VIL AND THE ANTI-CHRIST.
WHAT'LL IT BE?
UH...I THINK I'LL HAVE THE BANANA SPLIT SUPREME, PLEASE.
ARE YOU SURE YOU CAN HANDLE ALL THAT ICE CREAM ON YOUR OWN? USUALLY TAKES ME AND MY DAUGHTER...
I'M CELEBRATING!
JUST SOLD MY FIRST SONG, AND NONE OTHER THAN DANA DARLING'S GOING TO RECORD IT!
OH, SO YOU'RE A SONGWRITER?

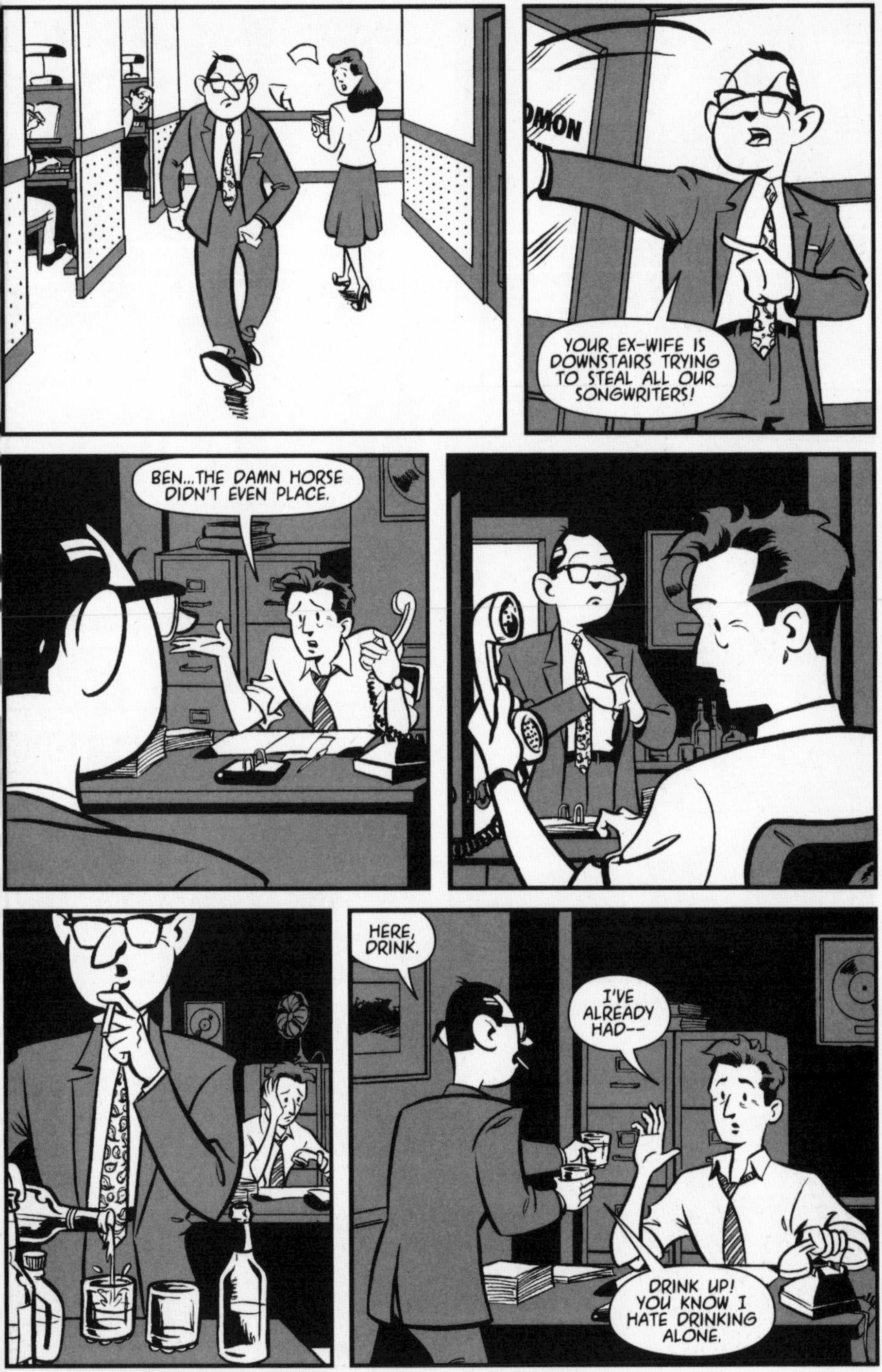
OMON
YOUR EX-WIFE IS DOWNSTAIRS TRYING TO STEAL ALL OUR SONGWRITERS!
BEN...THE DAMN HORSE DIDN'T EVEN PLACE.
HERE, DRINK.
I'VE ALREADY HAD--
DRINK UP! YOU KNOW I HATE DRINKING ALONE.

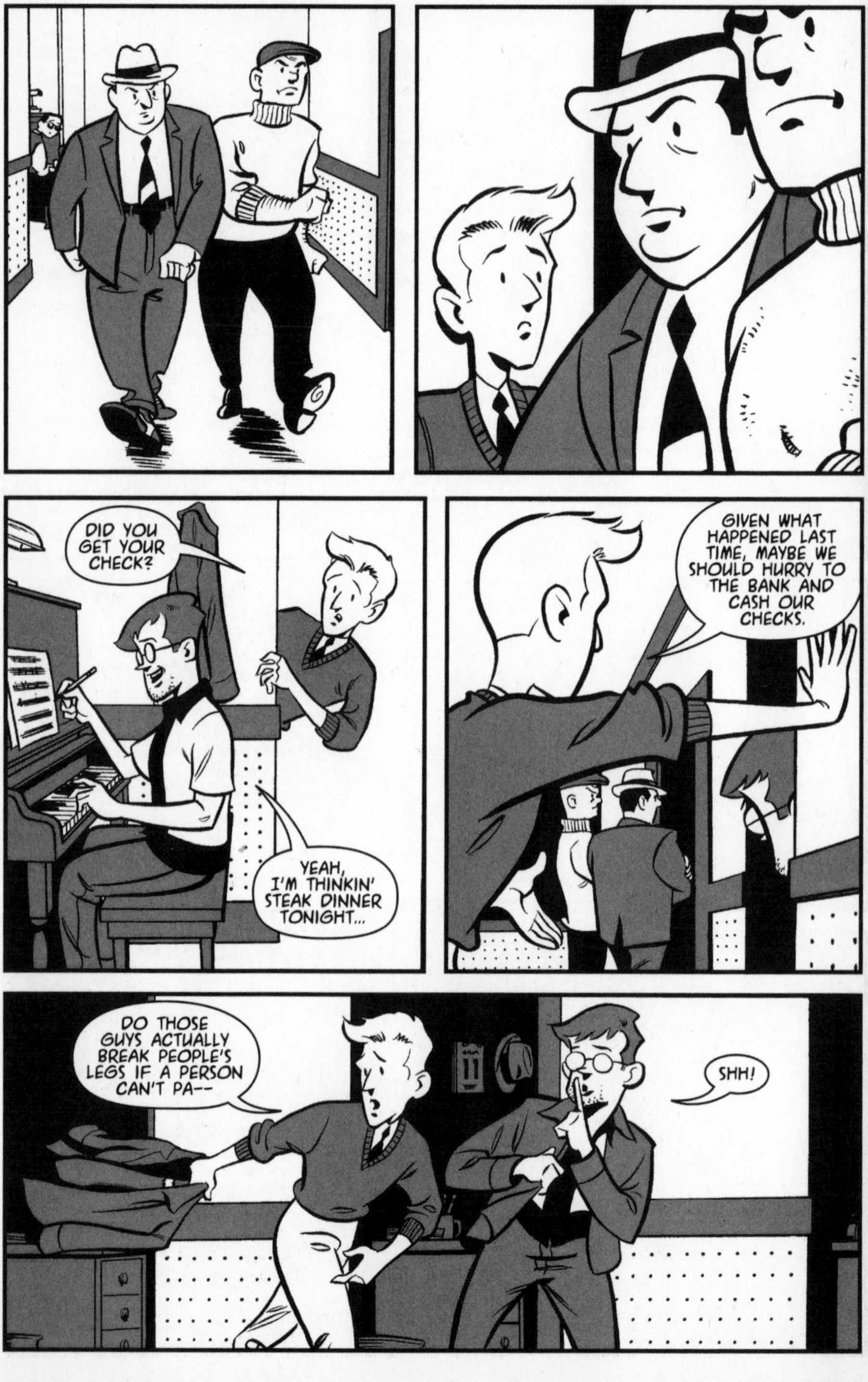
DID YOU GET YOUR CHECK?
YEAH, I'M THINKIN' STEAK DINNER TONIGHT...
GIVEN WHAT HAPPENED LAST TIME, MAYBE WE SHOULD HURRY TO THE BANK AND CASH OUR CHECKS.
DO THOSE GUYS ACTUALLY BREAK PEOPLE'S LEGS IF A PERSON CAN'T PA--
SHH!

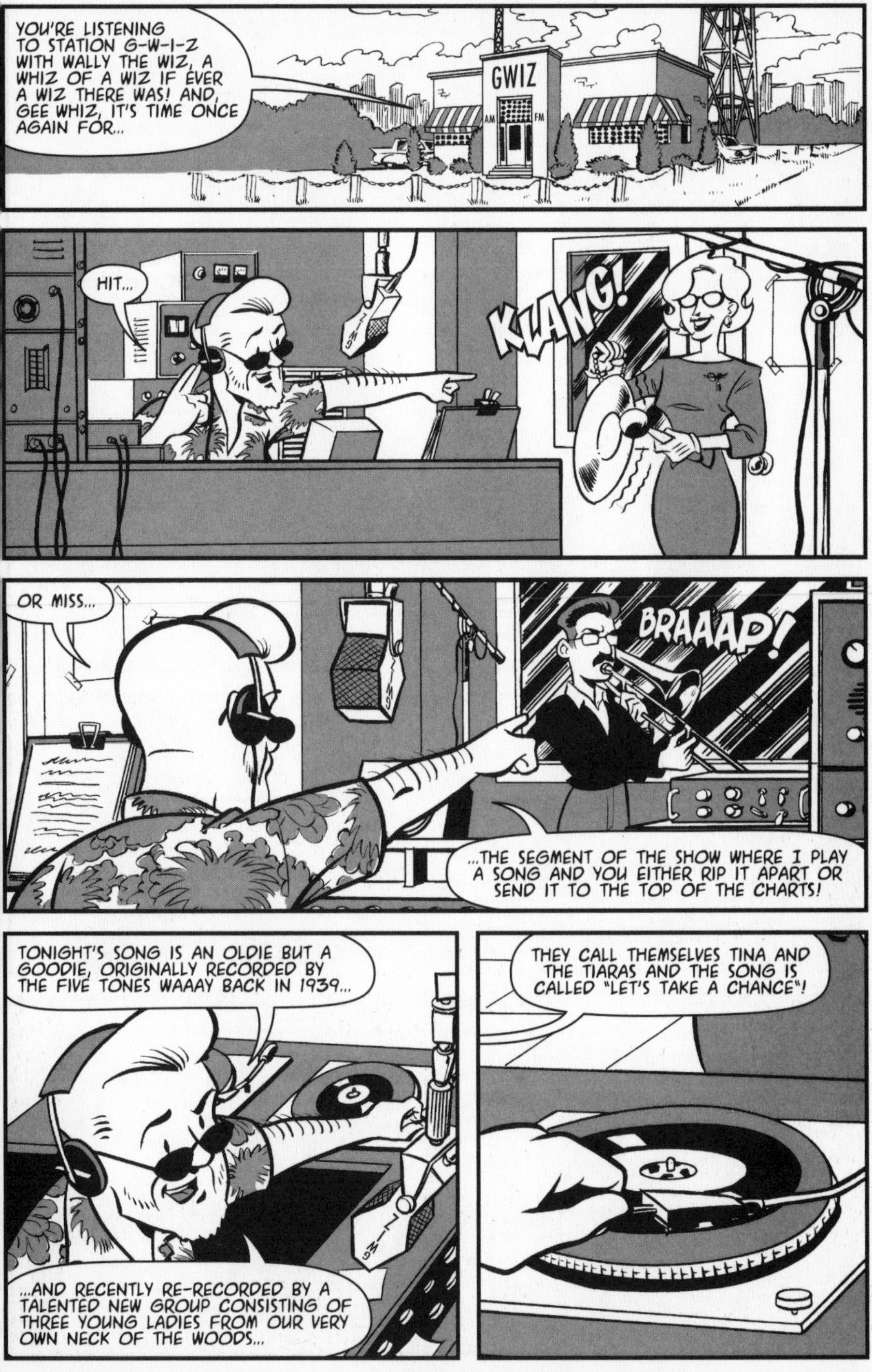

YOU'RE LISTENING TO STATION G-W-I-Z WITH WALLY THE WIZ, A WHIZ OF A WIZ IF EVER A WIZ THERE WAS! AND, GEE WHIZ, IT'S TIME ONCE AGAIN FOR...
GWIZ
AM
FM
HIT...
KLANG!
OR MISS...
BRAAAP!
...THE SEGMENT OF THE SHOW WHERE I PLAY A SONG AND YOU EITHER RIP IT APART OR SEND IT TO THE TOP OF THE CHARTS!
TONIGHT'S SONG IS AN OLDIE BUT A GOODIE, ORIGINALLY RECORDED BY THE FIVE TONES WAAAY BACK IN 1939...
...AND RECENTLY RE-RECORDED BY A TALENTED NEW GROUP CONSISTING OF THREE YOUNG LADIES FROM OUR VERY OWN NECK OF THE WOODS...
THEY CALL THEMSELVES TINA AND THE TIARAS AND THE SONG IS CALLED "LET'S TAKE A CHANCE"!

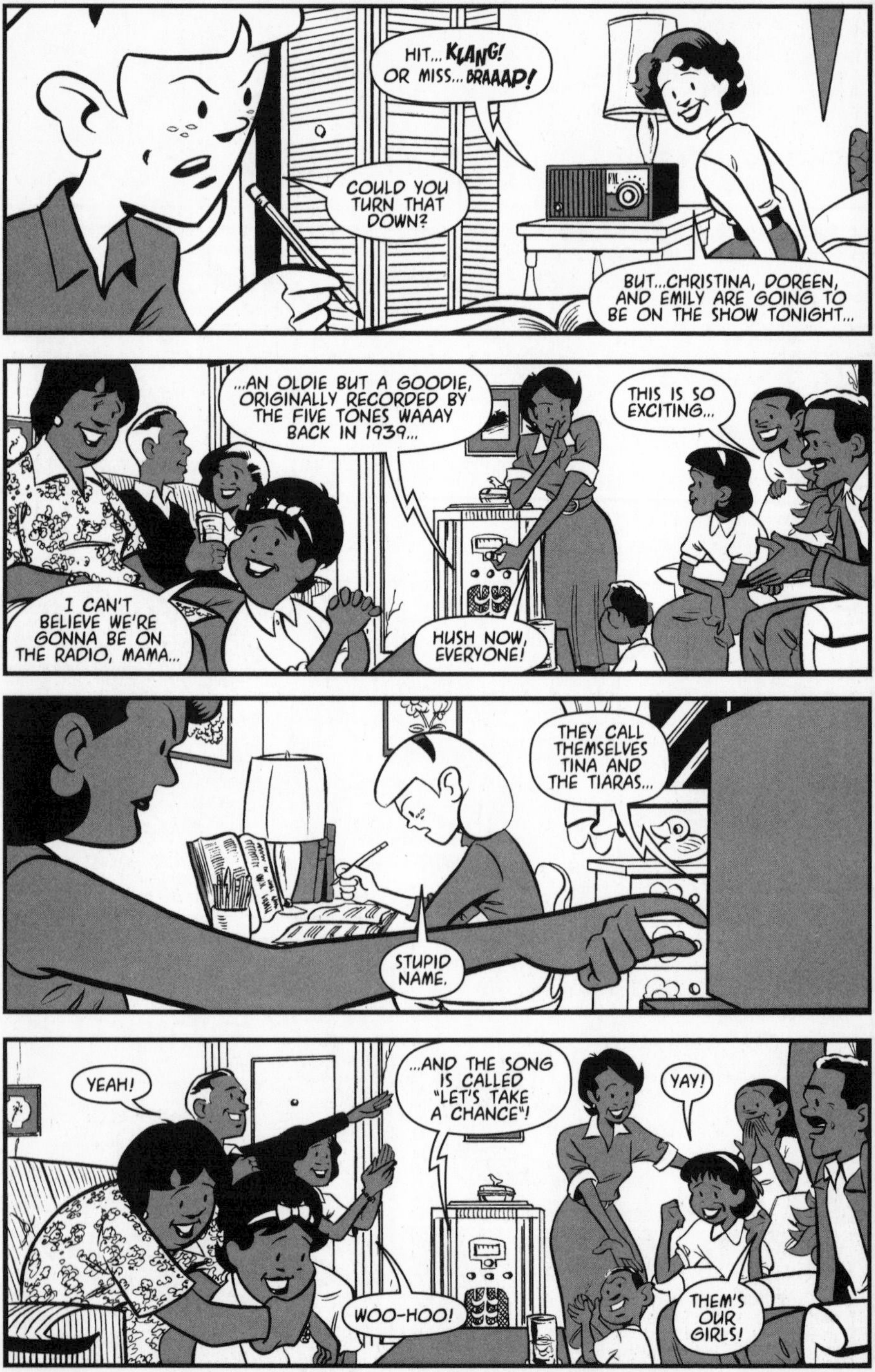
HIT... KLANG! OR MISS... BRAAAP!
COULD YOU TURN THAT DOWN?
BUT...CHRISTINA, DOREEN, AND EMILY ARE GOING TO BE ON THE SHOW TONIGHT...
...AN OLDIE BUT A GOODIE, ORIGINALLY RECORDED BY THE FIVE TONES WAAAY BACK IN 1939...
THIS IS SO EXCITING...
I CAN'T BELIEVE WE'RE GONNA BE ON THE RADIO, MAMA...
HUSH NOW, EVERYONE!
THEY CALL THEMSELVES TINA AND THE TIARAS...
STUPID NAME.
YEAH!
...AND THE SONG IS CALLED "LET'S TAKE A CHANCE"!
YAY!
WOO-HOO!
THEM'S OUR GIRLS!

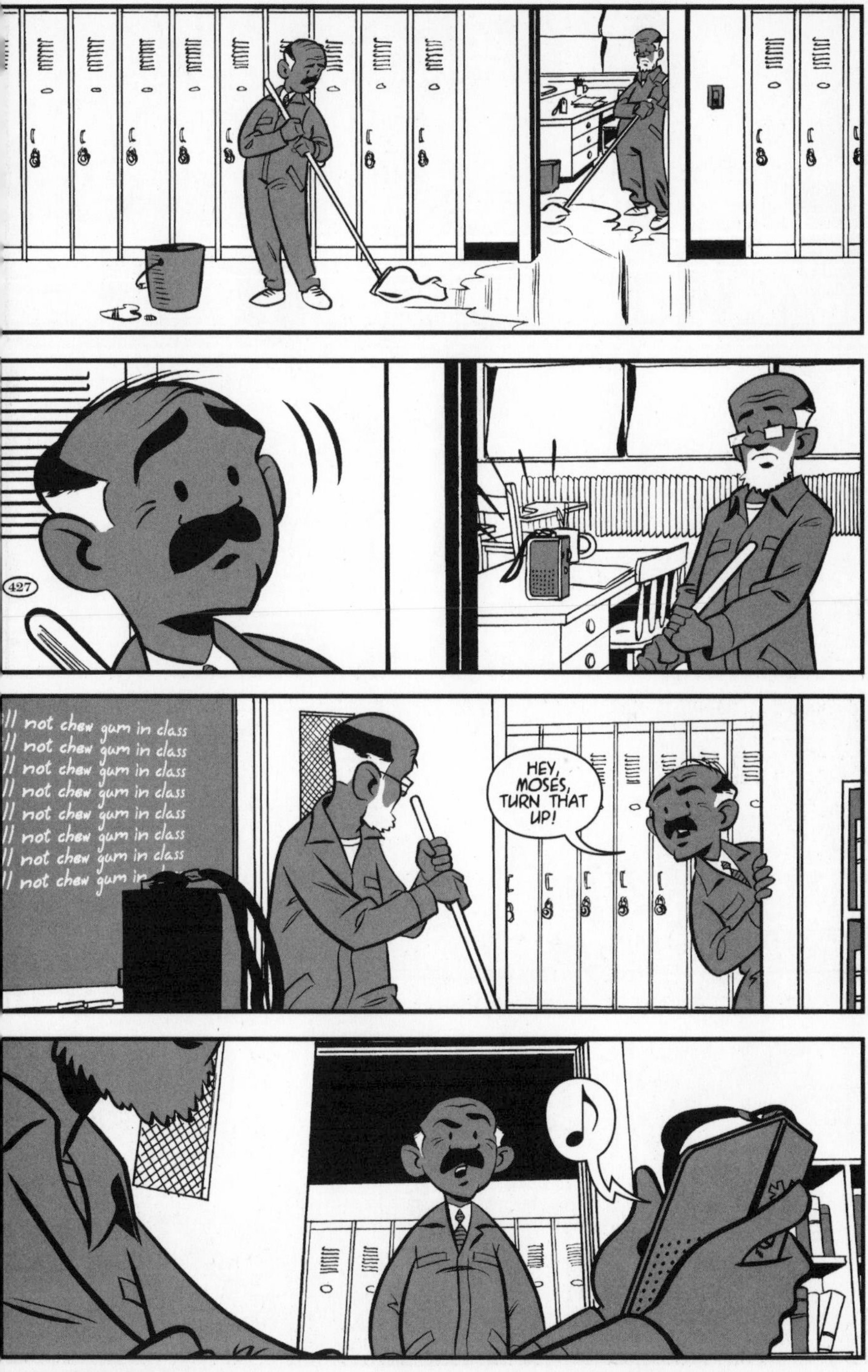
ll not chew gum in class
ll not chew gum in class
ll not chew gum in class
ll not chew gum in class
ll not chew gum in class
ll not chew gum in class
ll not chew gum in class
ll not chew gum in
HEY, MOSES, TURN THAT UP!

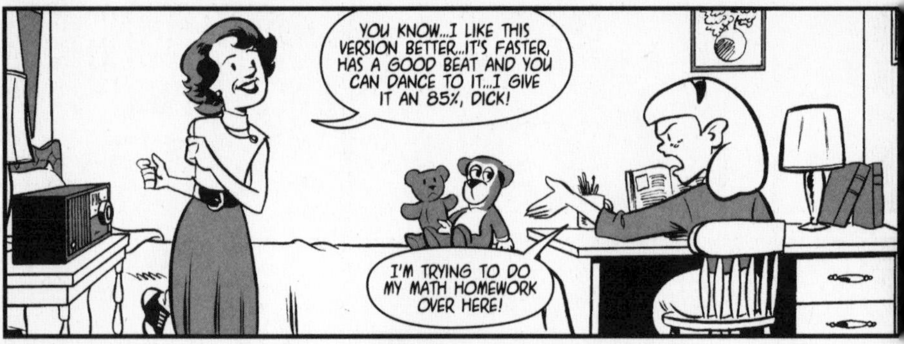
YOU KNOW...I LIKE THIS VERSION BETTER...IT'S FASTER, HAS A GOOD BEAT AND YOU CAN DANCE TO IT...I GIVE IT AN 85%, DICK!
I'M TRYING TO DO MY MATH HOMEWORK OVER HERE!
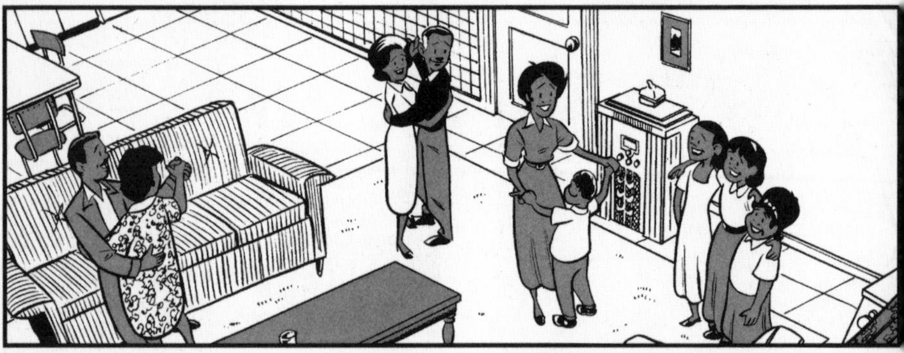
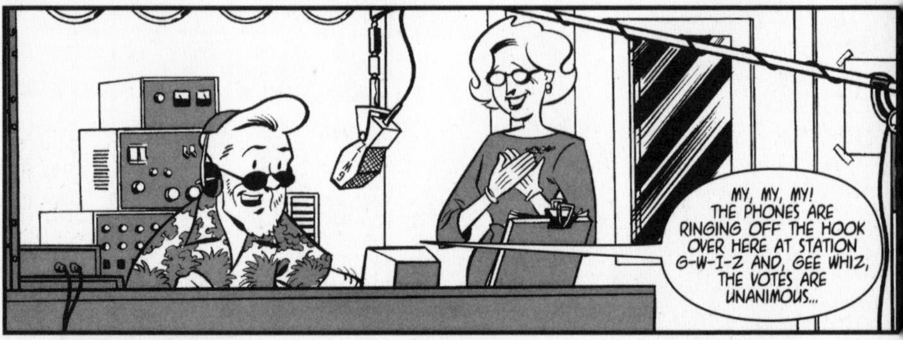
MY, MY, MY! THE PHONES ARE RINGING OFF THE HOOK OVER HERE AT STATION G-W-I-Z AND, GEE WHIZ, THE VOTES ARE UNANIMOUS...
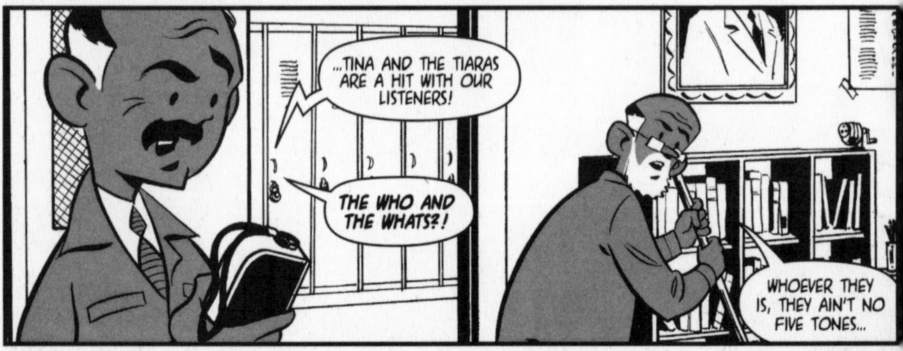
...TINA AND THE TIARAS ARE A HIT WITH OUR LISTENERS!
THE WHO AND THE WHATS?!
WHOEVER THEY IS, THEY AIN'T NO FIVE TONES...

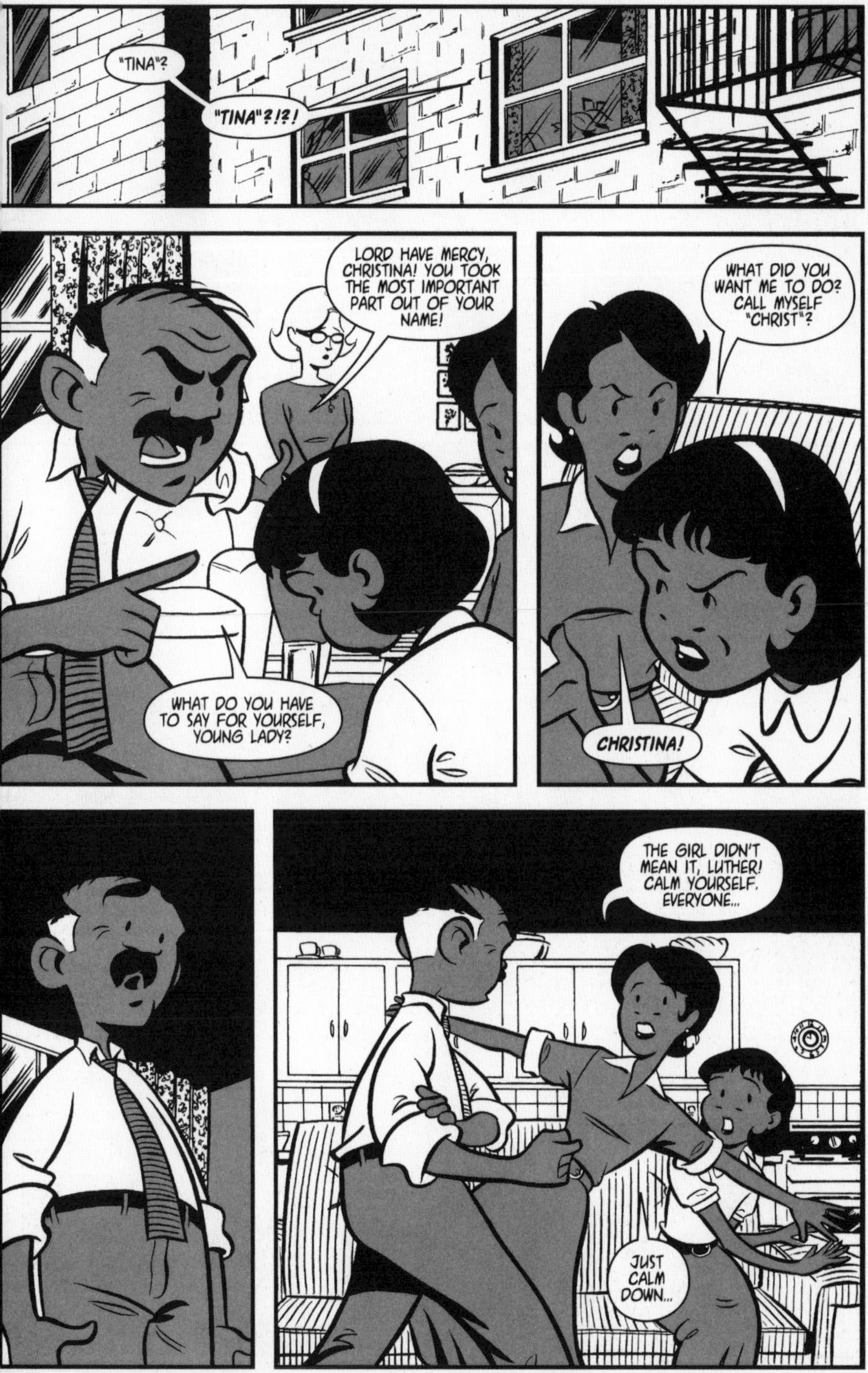
"TINA"?
"TINA"?!?!
LORD HAVE MERCY, CHRISTINA! YOU TOOK THE MOST IMPORTANT PART OUT OF YOUR NAME!
WHAT DO YOU HAVE TO SAY FOR YOURSELF, YOUNG LADY?
WHAT DID YOU WANT ME TO DO? CALL MYSELF "CHRIST"?
CHRISTINA!
THE GIRL DIDN'T MEAN IT, LUTHER! CALM YOURSELF. EVERYONE...
JUST CALM DOWN...

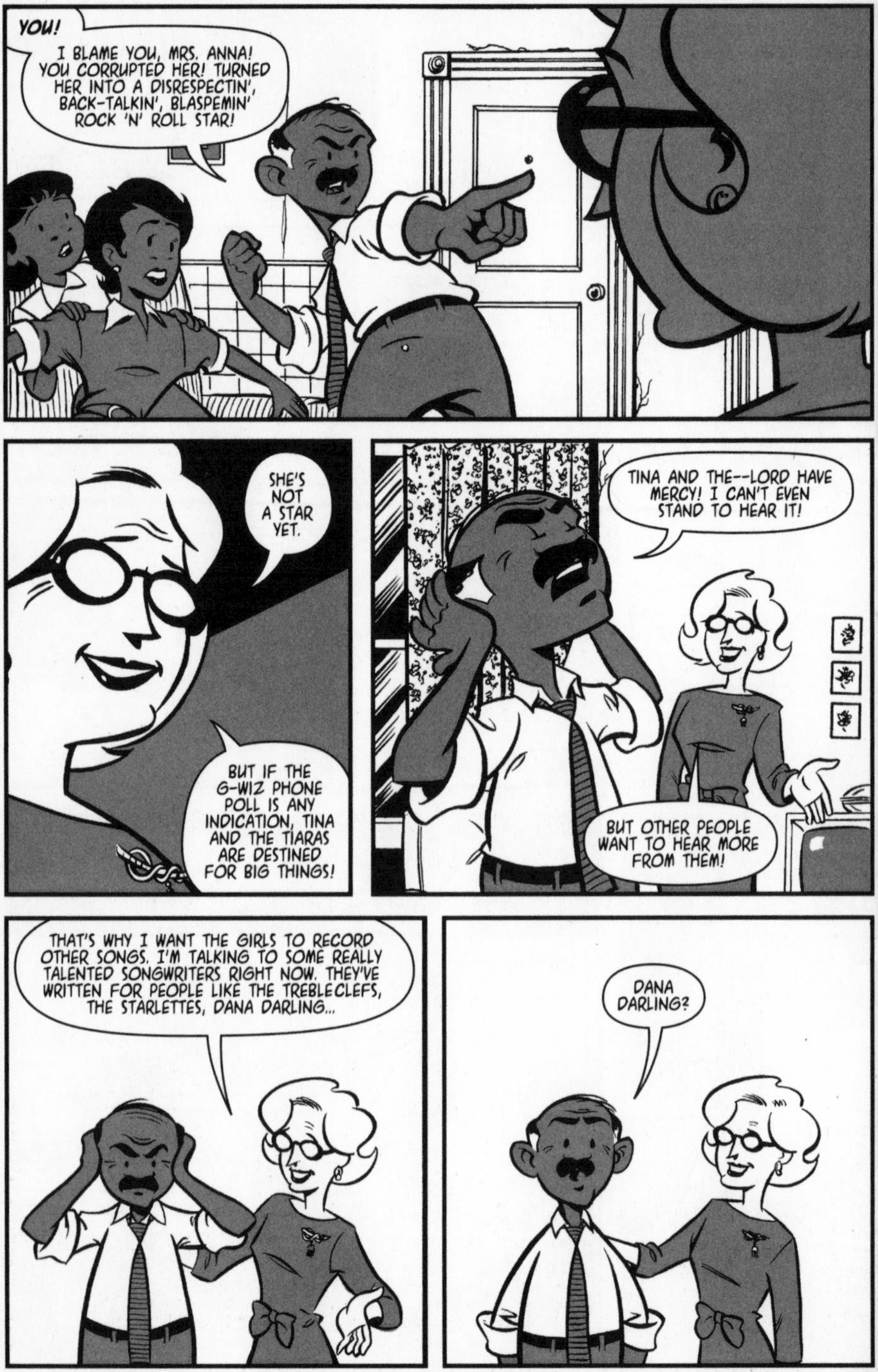
YOU!
I BLAME YOU, MRS. ANNA! YOU CORRUPTED HER! TURNED HER INTO A DISRESPECTIN', BACK-TALKIN', BLASPEMIN' ROCK 'N' ROLL STAR!
SHE'S NOT A STAR YET.
BUT IF THE G-WIZ PHONE POLL IS ANY INDICATION, TINA AND THE TIARAS ARE DESTINED FOR BIG THINGS!
TINA AND THE--LORD HAVE MERCY! I CAN'T EVEN STAND TO HEAR IT!
BUT OTHER PEOPLE WANT TO HEAR MORE FROM THEM!
THAT'S WHY I WANT THE GIRLS TO RECORD OTHER SONGS. I'M TALKING TO SOME REALLY TALENTED SONGWRITERS RIGHT NOW. THEY'VE WRITTEN FOR PEOPLE LIKE THE TREBLECLEFS, THE STARLETTES, DANA DARLING...
DANA DARLING?

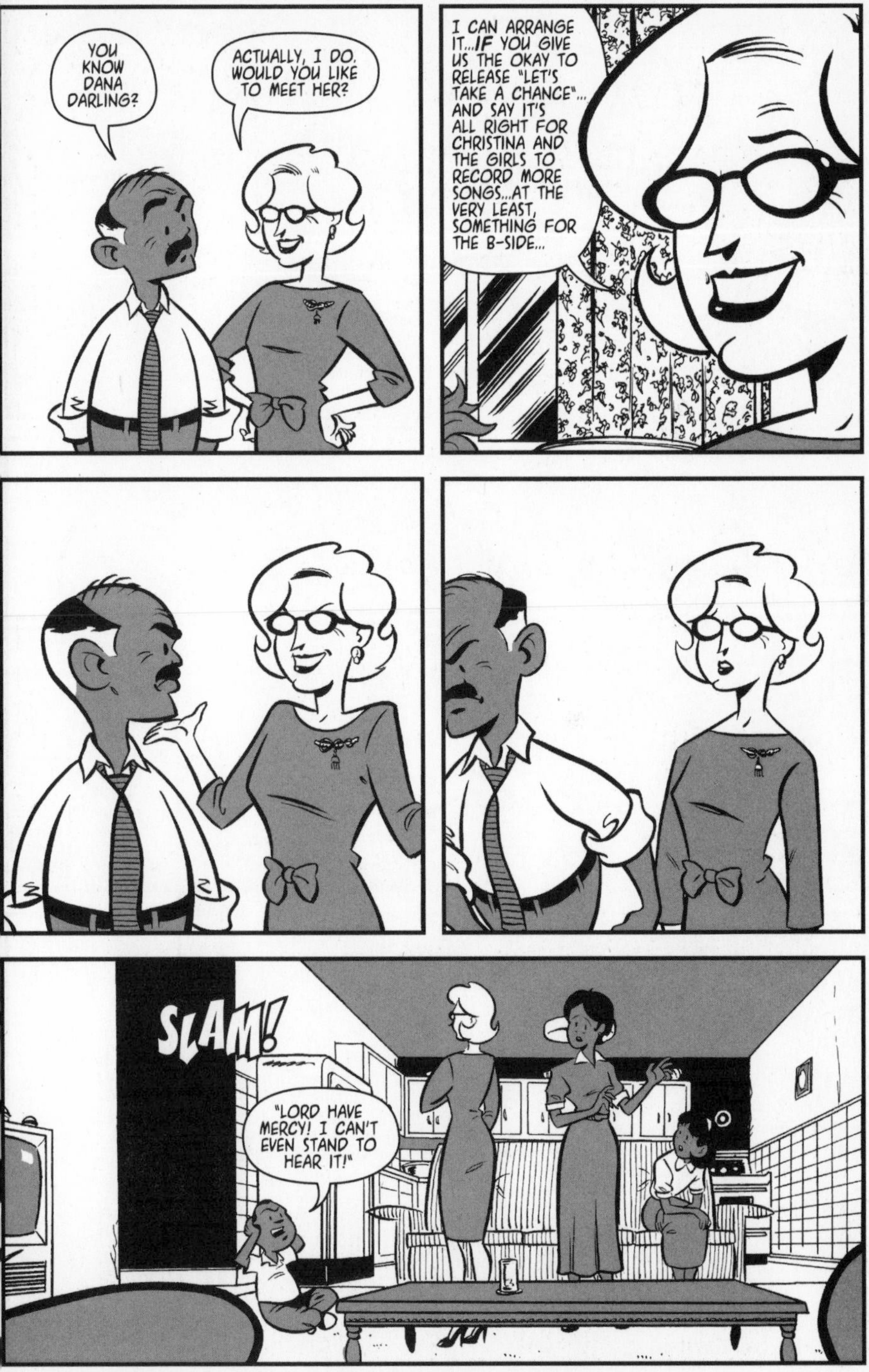
YOU KNOW DANA DARLING?
ACTUALLY, I DO. WOULD YOU LIKE TO MEET HER?
I CAN ARRANGE IT...**IF** YOU GIVE US THE OKAY TO RELEASE "LET'S TAKE A CHANCE"... AND SAY IT'S ALL RIGHT FOR CHRISTINA AND THE GIRLS TO RECORD MORE SONGS...AT THE VERY LEAST, SOMETHING FOR THE B-SIDE...
SLAM!
"LORD HAVE MERCY! I CAN'T EVEN STAND TO HEAR IT!"

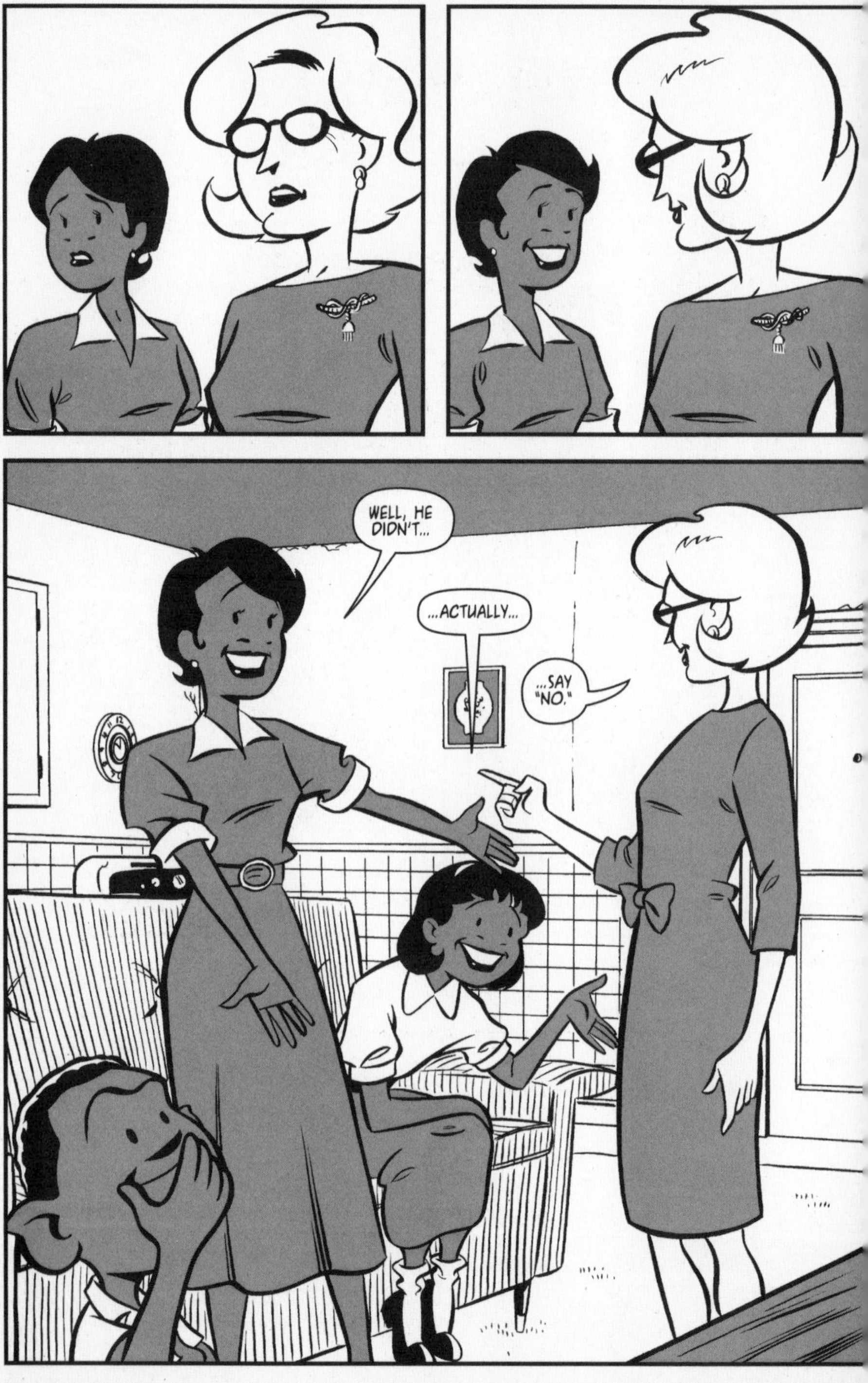
WELL, HE DIDN'T...
...ACTUALLY...
...SAY "NO."

CHAPTER 3
"Tonight's The Night"

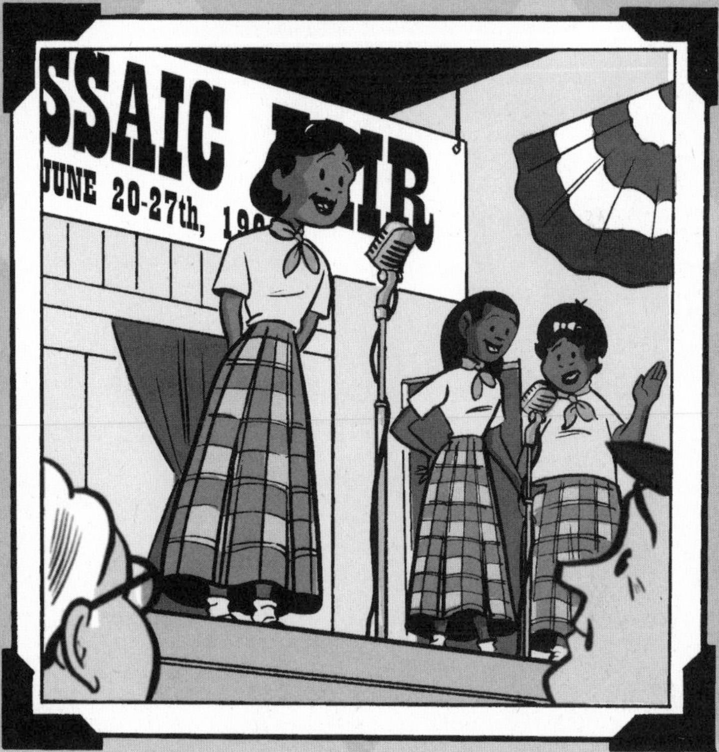

SSAIC
JUNE 20-27th, 19

"Passaic Fair. Getting ready to perform."

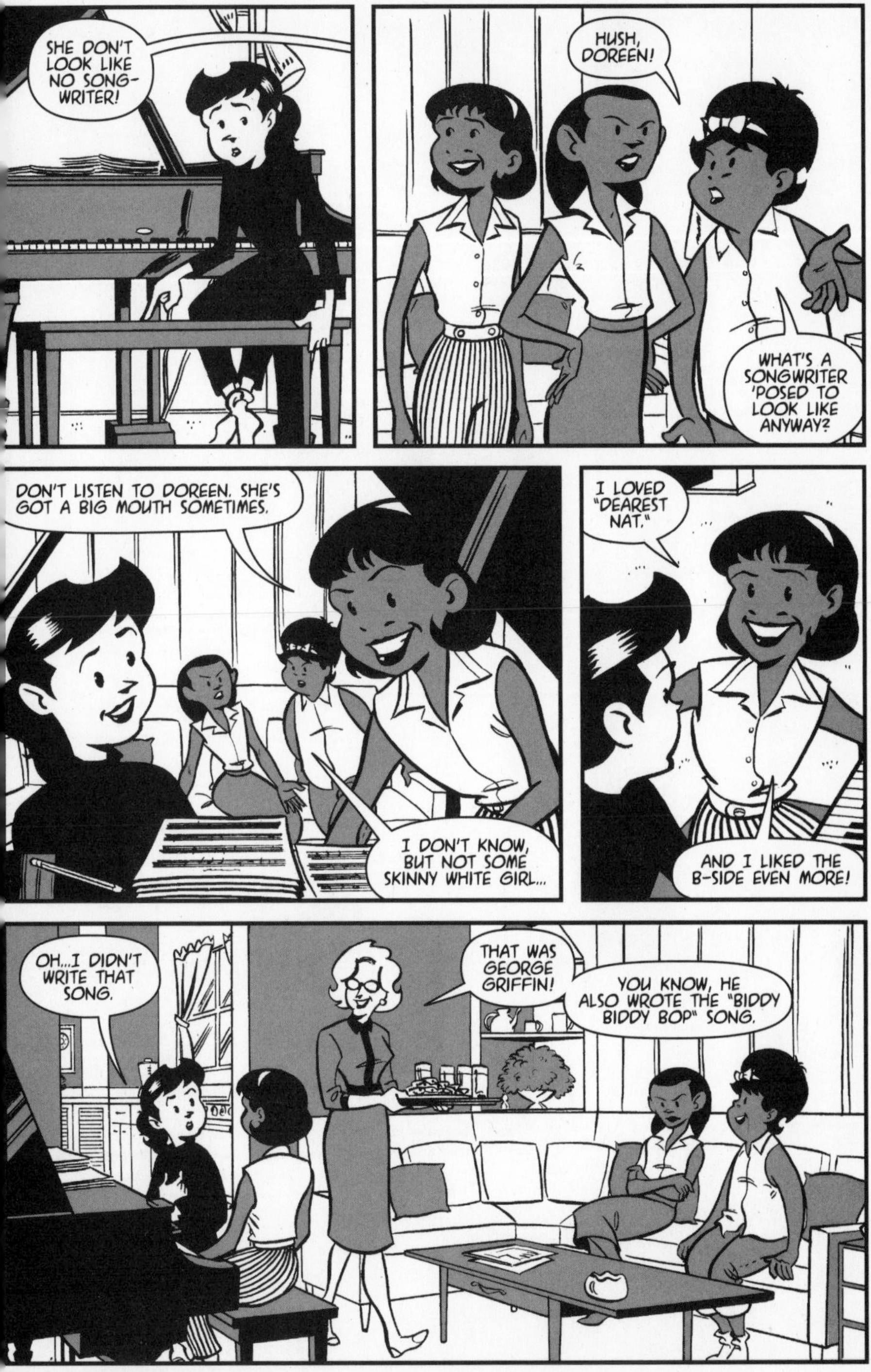
SHE DON'T LOOK LIKE NO SONG-WRITER!
HUSH, DOREEN!
WHAT'S A SONGWRITER 'POSED TO LOOK LIKE ANYWAY?
DON'T LISTEN TO DOREEN. SHE'S GOT A BIG MOUTH SOMETIMES.
I DON'T KNOW, BUT NOT SOME SKINNY WHITE GIRL...
I LOVED "DEAREST NAT."
AND I LIKED THE B-SIDE EVEN MORE!
OH...I DIDN'T WRITE THAT SONG.
THAT WAS GEORGE GRIFFIN!
YOU KNOW, HE ALSO WROTE THE "BIDDY BIDDY BOP" SONG.

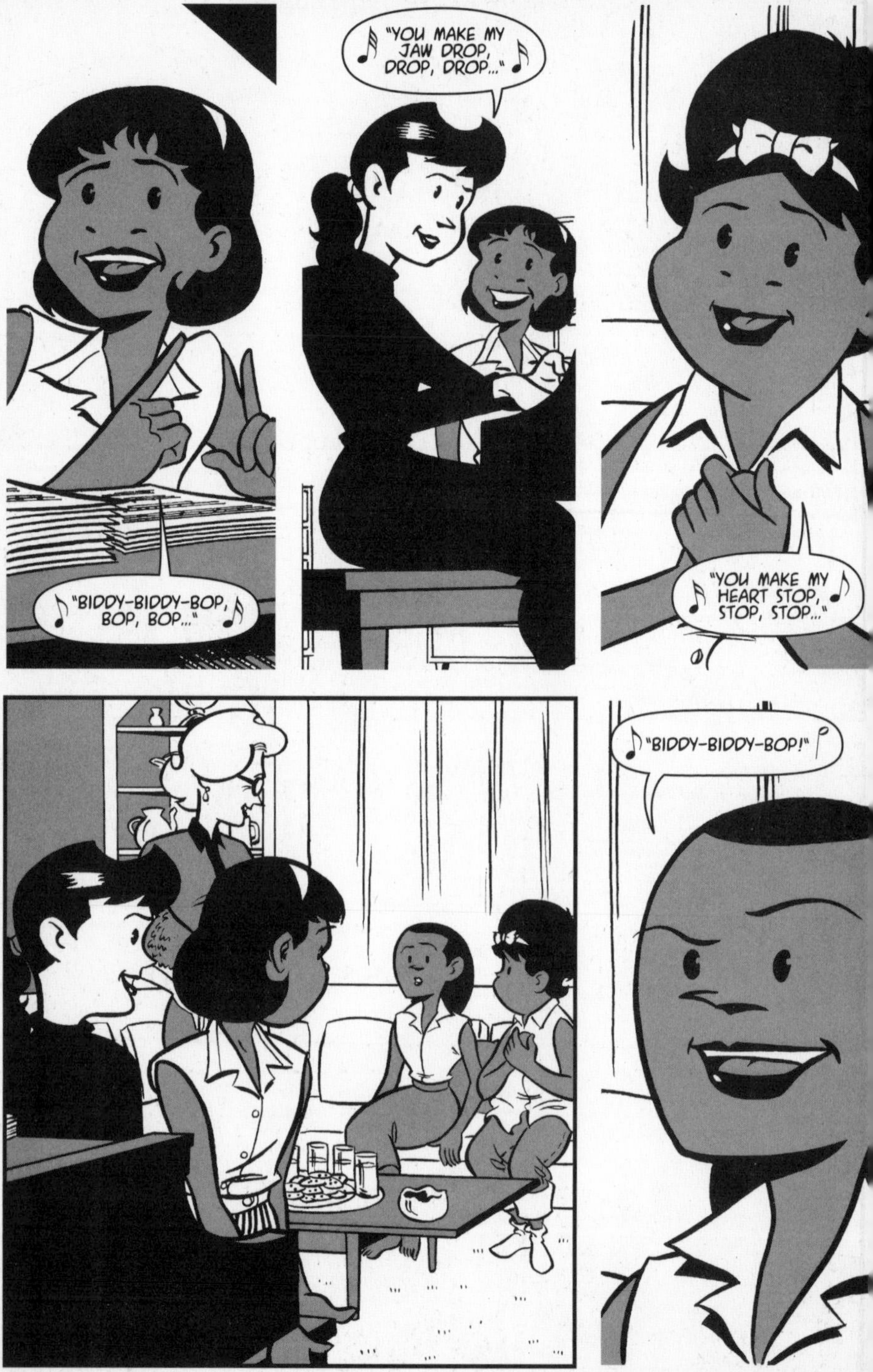
"BIDDY-BIDDY-BOP, BOP, BOP..."
"YOU MAKE MY JAW DROP, DROP, DROP..."
"YOU MAKE MY HEART STOP, STOP, STOP..."
"BIDDY-BIDDY-BOP!"

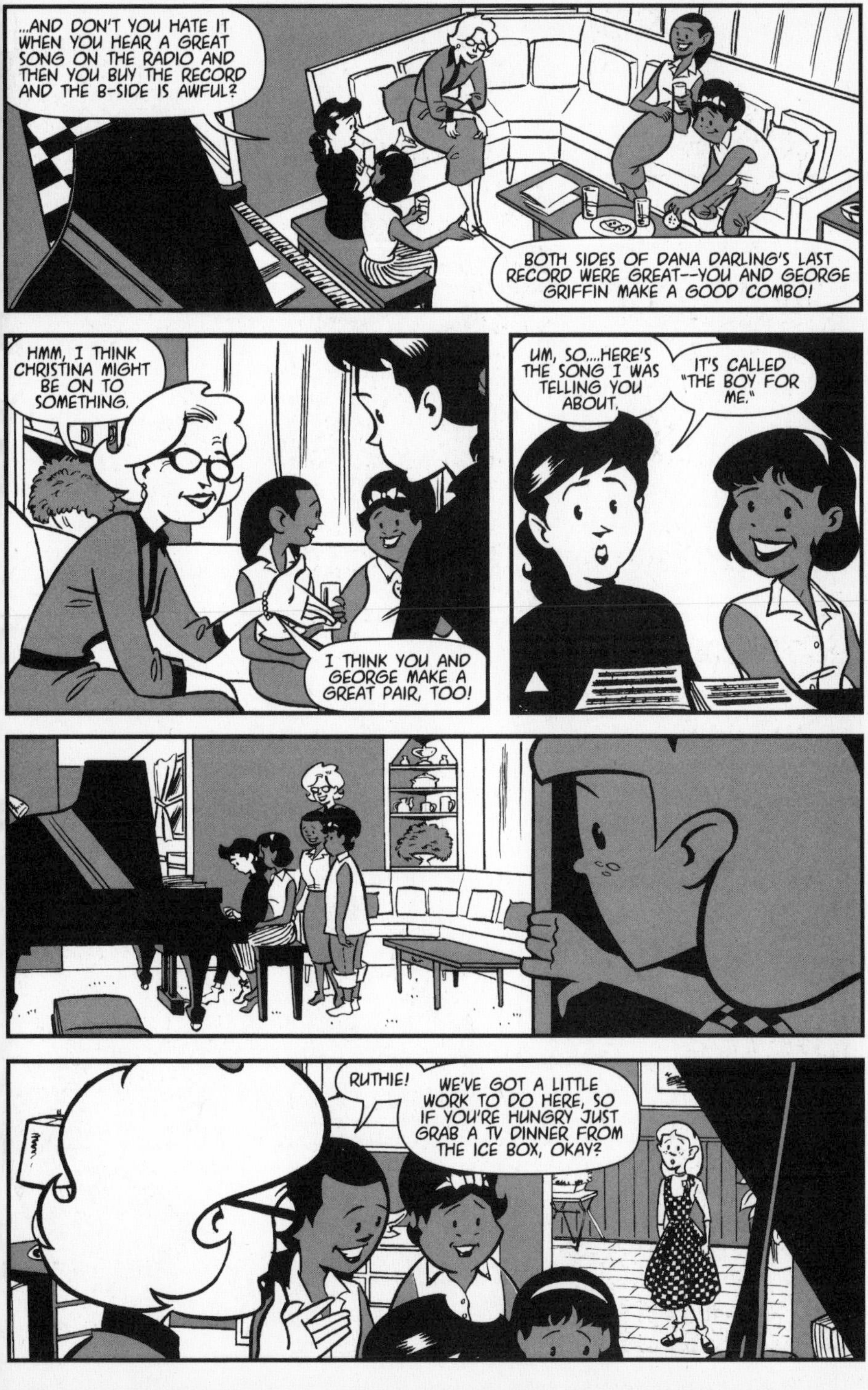
...AND DON'T YOU HATE IT WHEN YOU HEAR A GREAT SONG ON THE RADIO AND THEN YOU BUY THE RECORD AND THE B-SIDE IS AWFUL?
BOTH SIDES OF DANA DARLING'S LAST RECORD WERE GREAT--YOU AND GEORGE GRIFFIN MAKE A GOOD COMBO!
HMM, I THINK CHRISTINA MIGHT BE ON TO SOMETHING.
I THINK YOU AND GEORGE MAKE A GREAT PAIR, TOO!
UM, SO....HERE'S THE SONG I WAS TELLING YOU ABOUT.
IT'S CALLED "THE BOY FOR ME."
RUTHIE!
WE'VE GOT A LITTLE WORK TO DO HERE, SO IF YOU'RE HUNGRY JUST GRAB A TV DINNER FROM THE ICE BOX, OKAY?

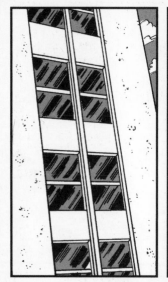

GUESS WHAT I JUST FOUND OUT!

TOMORROW'S CHARTS WILL SHOW YOUR WIFE'S LITTLE GIRL GROUP DEBUTING AT NUMBER 87! THAT'S JUST UNDER THE NEW MEDLEY BROTHERS SONG!

THE MEDLEYS...

...SIGH...

...IF ONLY YOU HAD LISTENED TO ME, ABE. THEY COULD'VE BEEN ON OUR LABEL.

YOU'RE REMEMBERING THINGS BACKWARDS AGAIN, BENJAMIN. I WANTED TO SIGN THEM, YOU'RE THE ONE WHO SAID THEY WERE A COUPLE OF BEATNIKS YOU COULDN'T TRUST.

WELL, WHATEVER THE CASE WE CAN'T LET SOME HOUSEWIFE SHOW US UP! I SAY, FIGHT FIRE WITH FIRE. WE NEED TO START UP OUR OWN GIRL GROUP!

GOOD IDEA, BUT YOU MIGHT HAVE TO CHECK WITH DIAMOND PICTURES.

THEY'VE PUT IN A BID. THE LAWYERS SAY WE SHOULD TAKE IT.

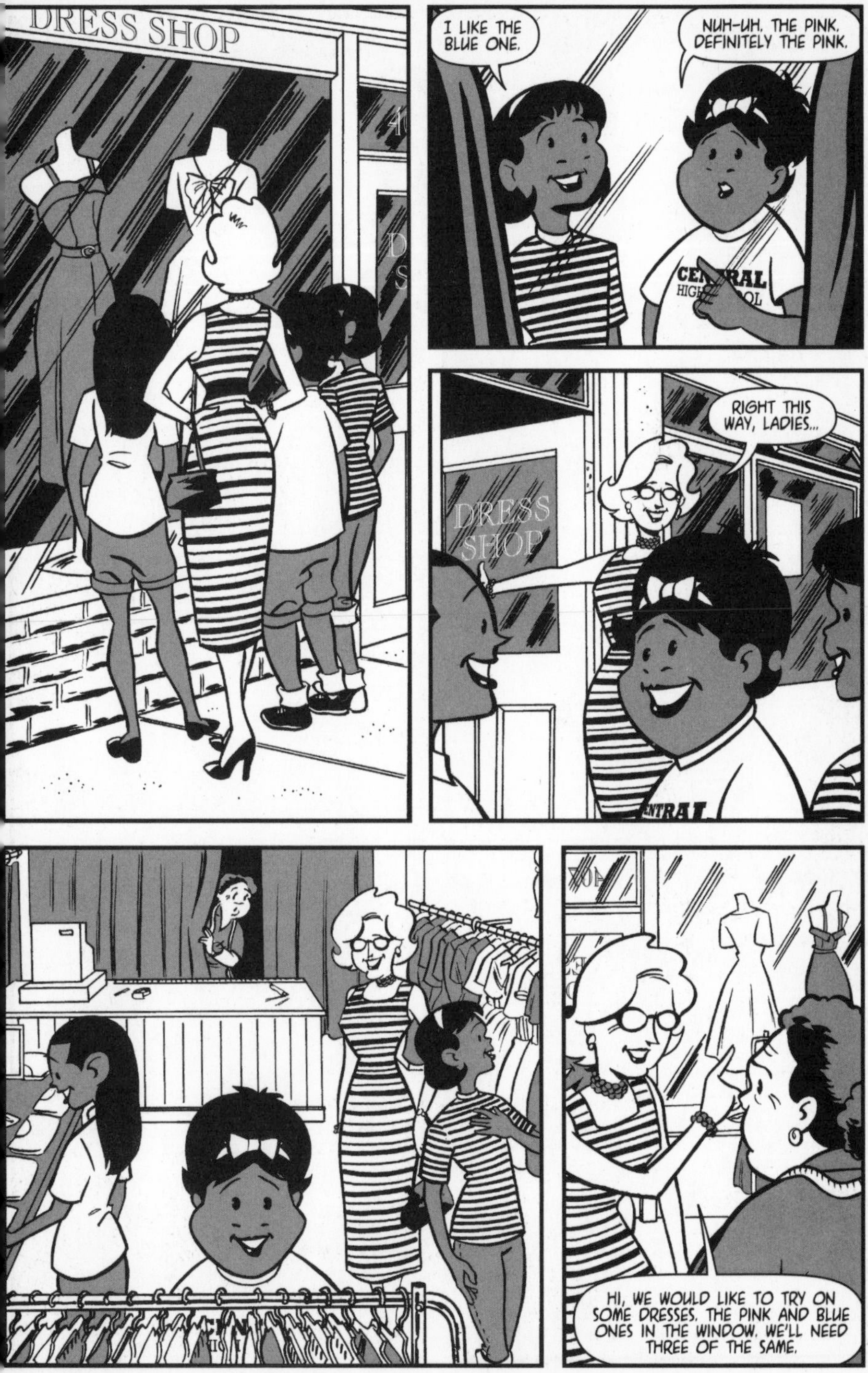
DRESS SHOP
I LIKE THE BLUE ONE.
NUH-UH. THE PINK. DEFINITELY THE PINK.
CENTRAL HIGH SCHOOL
RIGHT THIS WAY, LADIES...
DRESS SHOP
HI, WE WOULD LIKE TO TRY ON SOME DRESSES. THE PINK AND BLUE ONES IN THE WINDOW. WE'LL NEED THREE OF THE SAME.

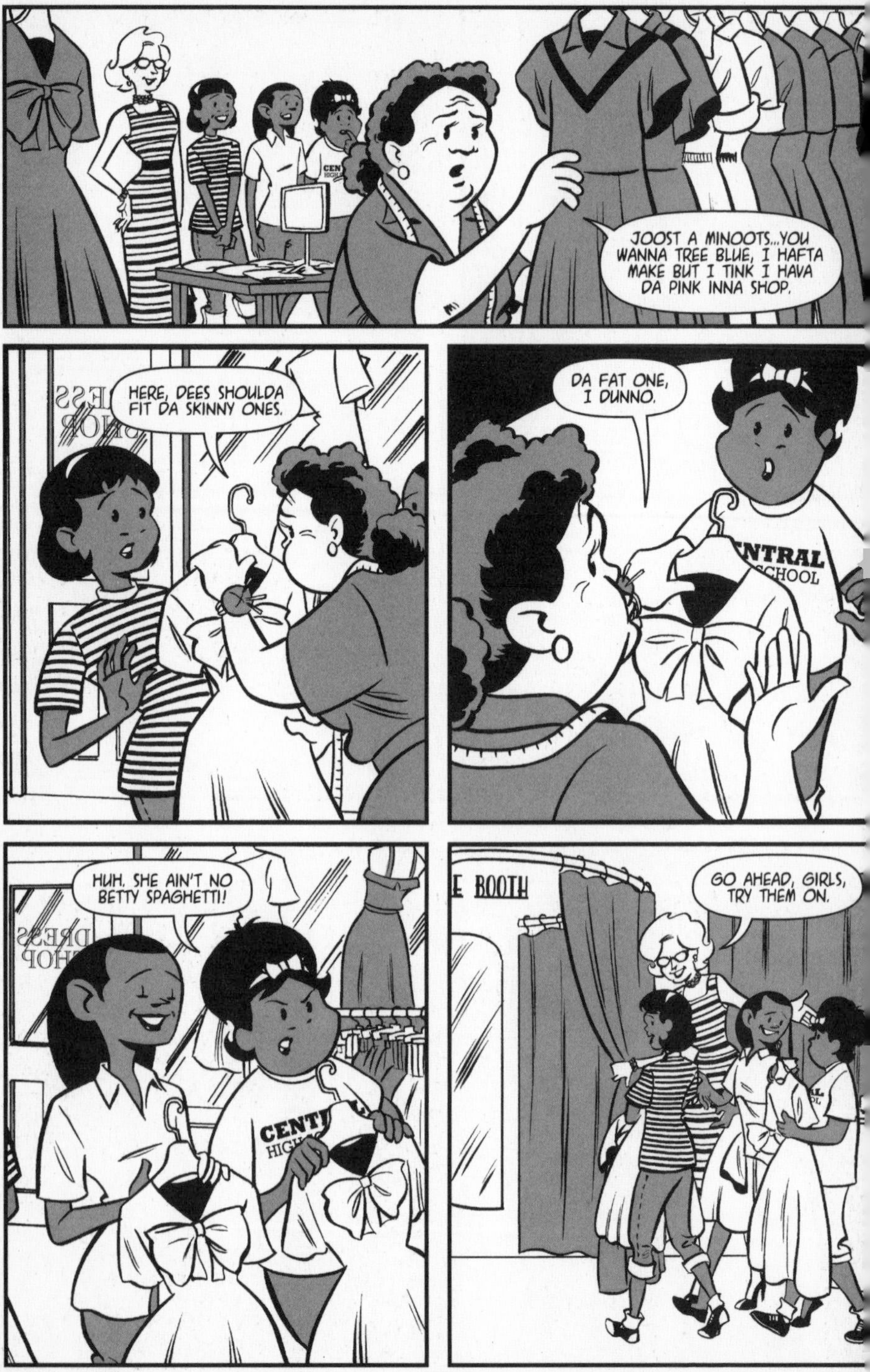
JOOST A MINOOTS...YOU WANNA TREE BLUE, I HAFTA MAKE BUT I TINK I HAVA DA PINK INNA SHOP.
HERE, DEES SHOULDA FIT DA SKINNY ONES.
DA FAT ONE, I DUNNO.
HUH. SHE AIN'T NO BETTY SPAGHETTI!
GO AHEAD, GIRLS, TRY THEM ON.

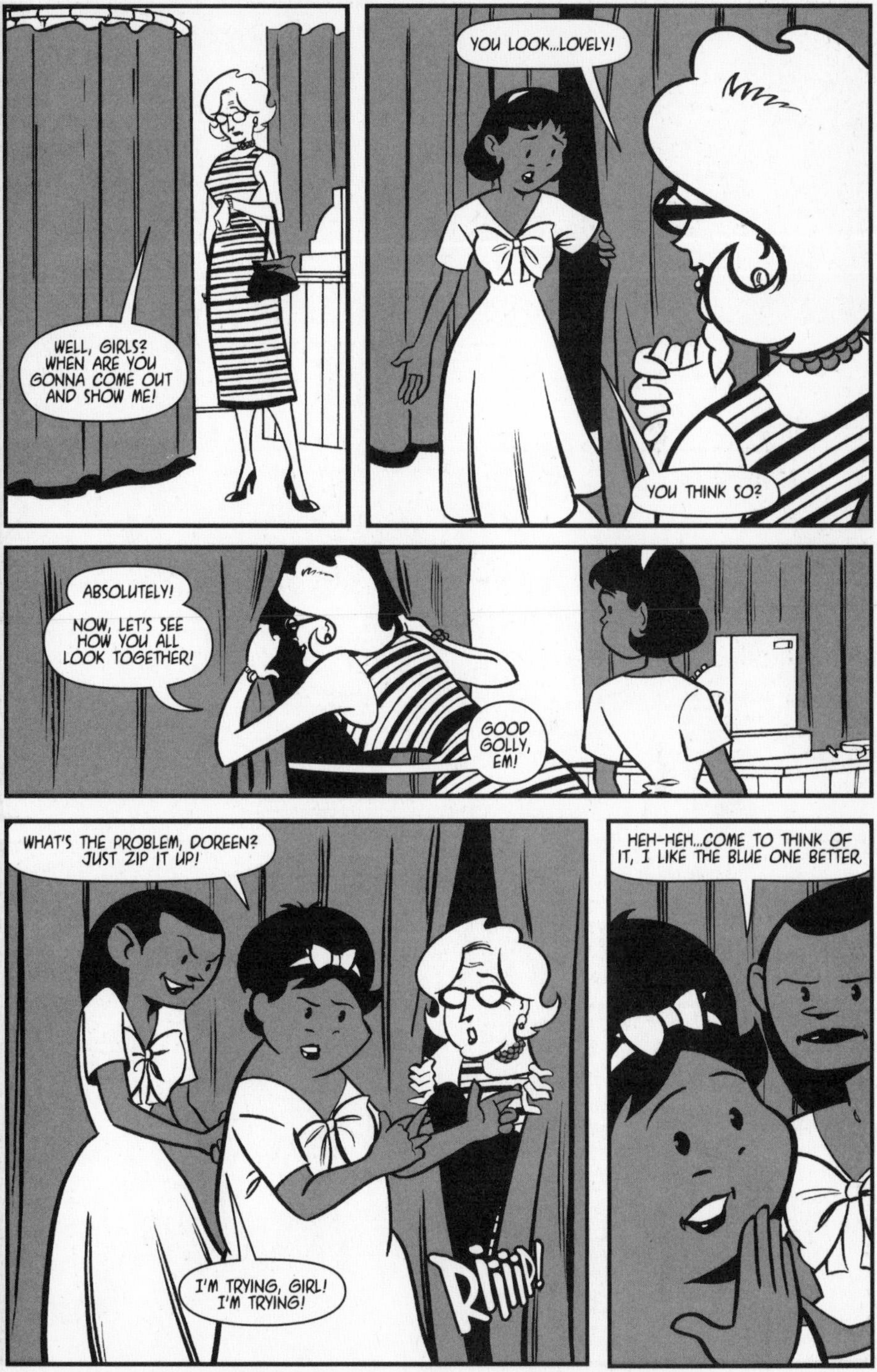
WELL, GIRLS? WHEN ARE YOU GONNA COME OUT AND SHOW ME!
YOU LOOK...LOVELY!
YOU THINK SO?
ABSOLUTELY!
NOW, LET'S SEE HOW YOU ALL LOOK TOGETHER!
GOOD GOLLY, EM!
WHAT'S THE PROBLEM, DOREEN? JUST ZIP IT UP!
I'M TRYING, GIRL! I'M TRYING!
RIIIIP!
HEH-HEH...COME TO THINK OF IT, I LIKE THE BLUE ONE BETTER.

OKAY, PIERRE, WE HAVE AN APPOINTMENT TO TAKE SOME PUBLICITY PICTURES THIS AFTERNOON.

Johnson's
BEAUTY PARLOR

JOHNSONS
BEAUTY PARLOR

SO, YOU'VE GOT ABOUT FOUR HOURS TO TURN MY GIRLS INTO GLAMOROUS WOMEN.

Look!

CENTRA
H SCHO

ANNA, I'M A HAIRDRESSER NOT A MIRACLE WORKER.

JUST JOSHING!

I HEARD "LET'S TAKE A CHANCE" ON THE RADIO THE OTHER DAY AND I LOVED IT! NOW, LET'S MAKE YOU LOOK AS DIVINE AS YOU SOUND...

EVERYONE WHO WANTS ME TO TURN THEM INTO LENA HORNE, WALK THIS WAY!

CENTRA
HIGH SCHO

WHO?

JUST GET YOUR NAPPY HEAD OVER THERE, EM!

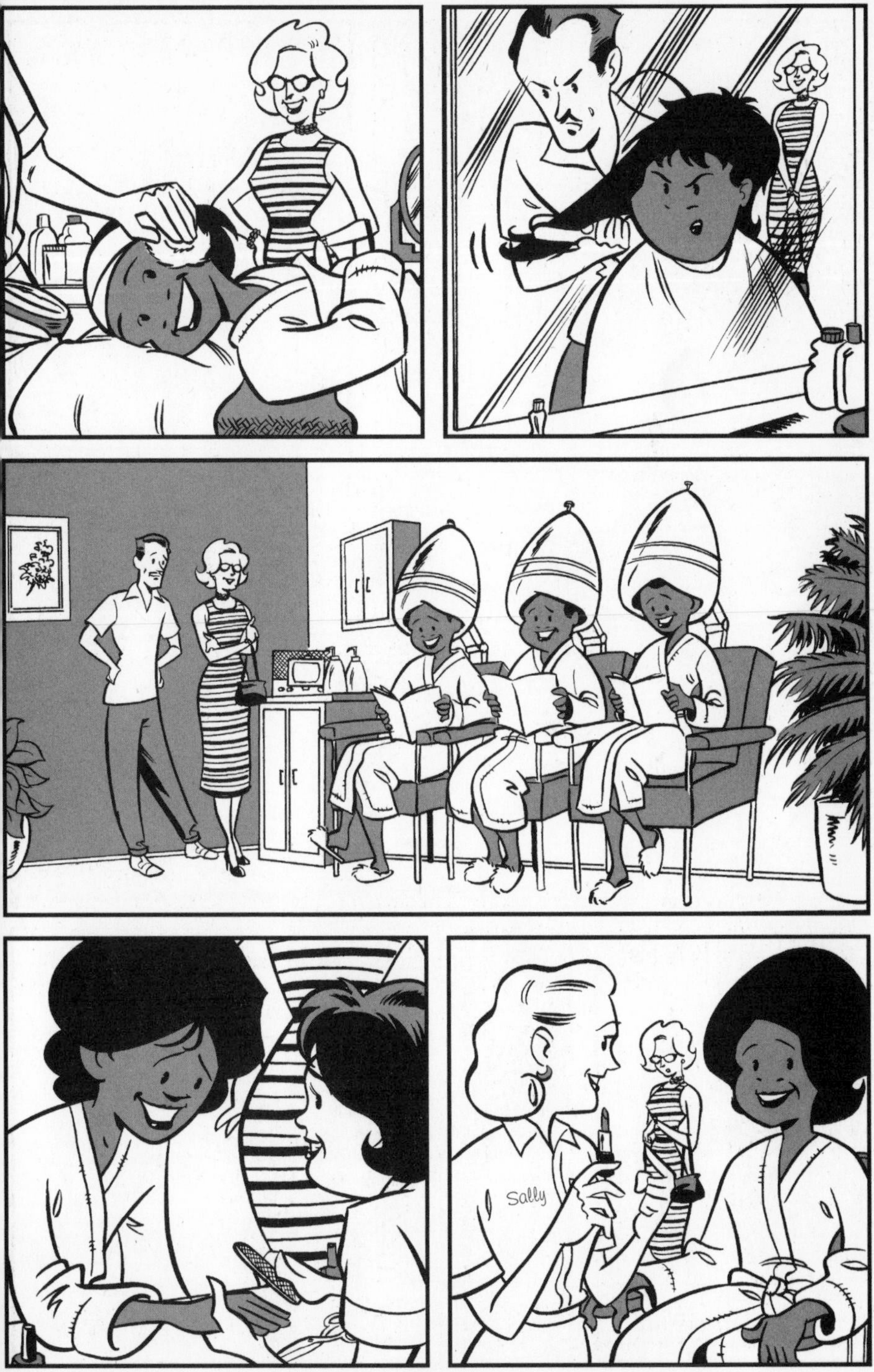
Sally

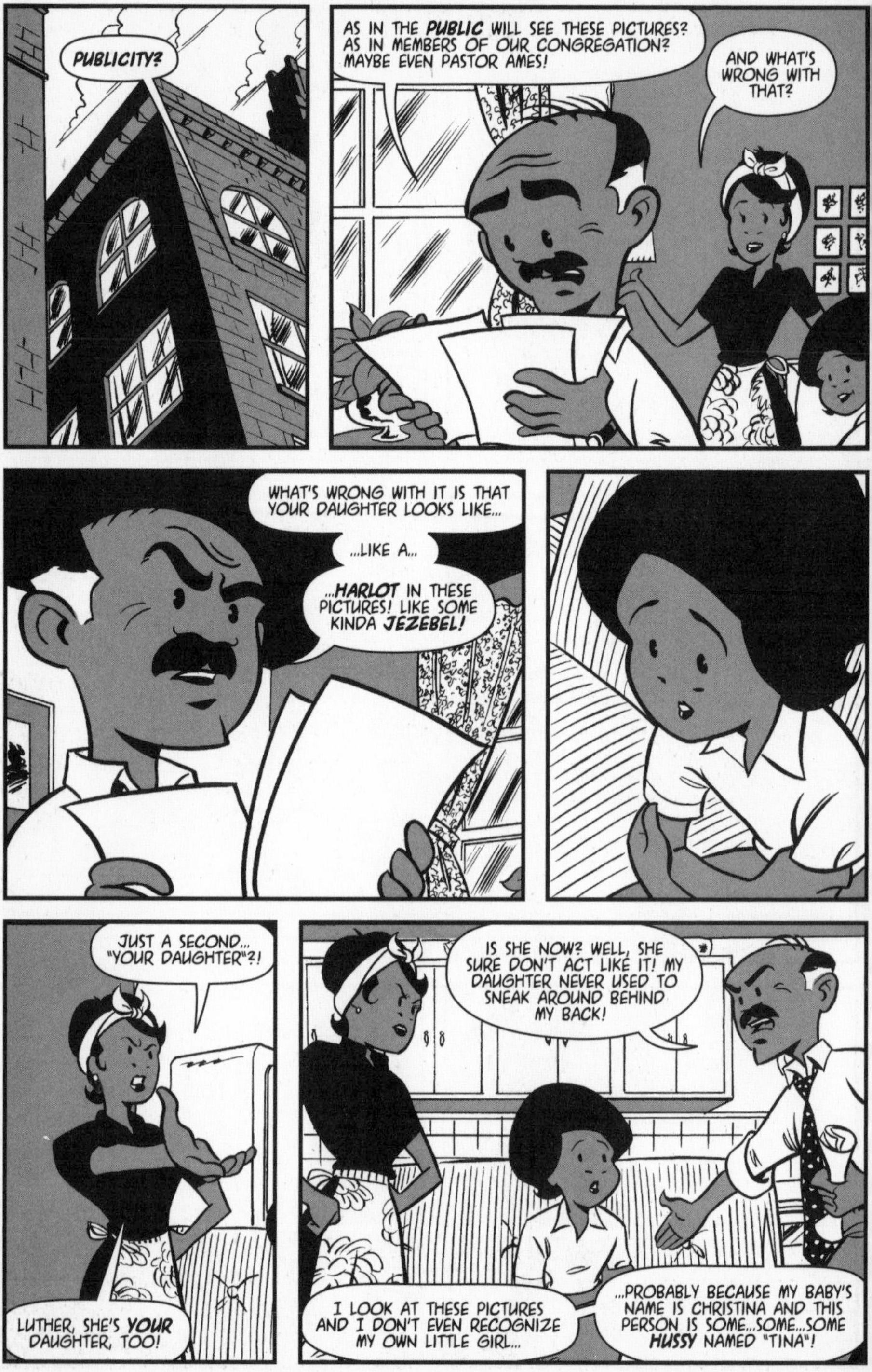
PUBLICITY?
AS IN THE PUBLIC WILL SEE THESE PICTURES? AS IN MEMBERS OF OUR CONGREGATION? MAYBE EVEN PASTOR AMES!
AND WHAT'S WRONG WITH THAT?
WHAT'S WRONG WITH IT IS THAT YOUR DAUGHTER LOOKS LIKE...
...LIKE A...
...HARLOT IN THESE PICTURES! LIKE SOME KINDA JEZEBEL!
JUST A SECOND... "YOUR DAUGHTER"?!
LUTHER, SHE'S YOUR DAUGHTER, TOO!
IS SHE NOW? WELL, SHE SURE DON'T ACT LIKE IT! MY DAUGHTER NEVER USED TO SNEAK AROUND BEHIND MY BACK!
I LOOK AT THESE PICTURES AND I DON'T EVEN RECOGNIZE MY OWN LITTLE GIRL...
...PROBABLY BECAUSE MY BABY'S NAME IS CHRISTINA AND THIS PERSON IS SOME...SOME...SOME HUSSY NAMED "TINA"!

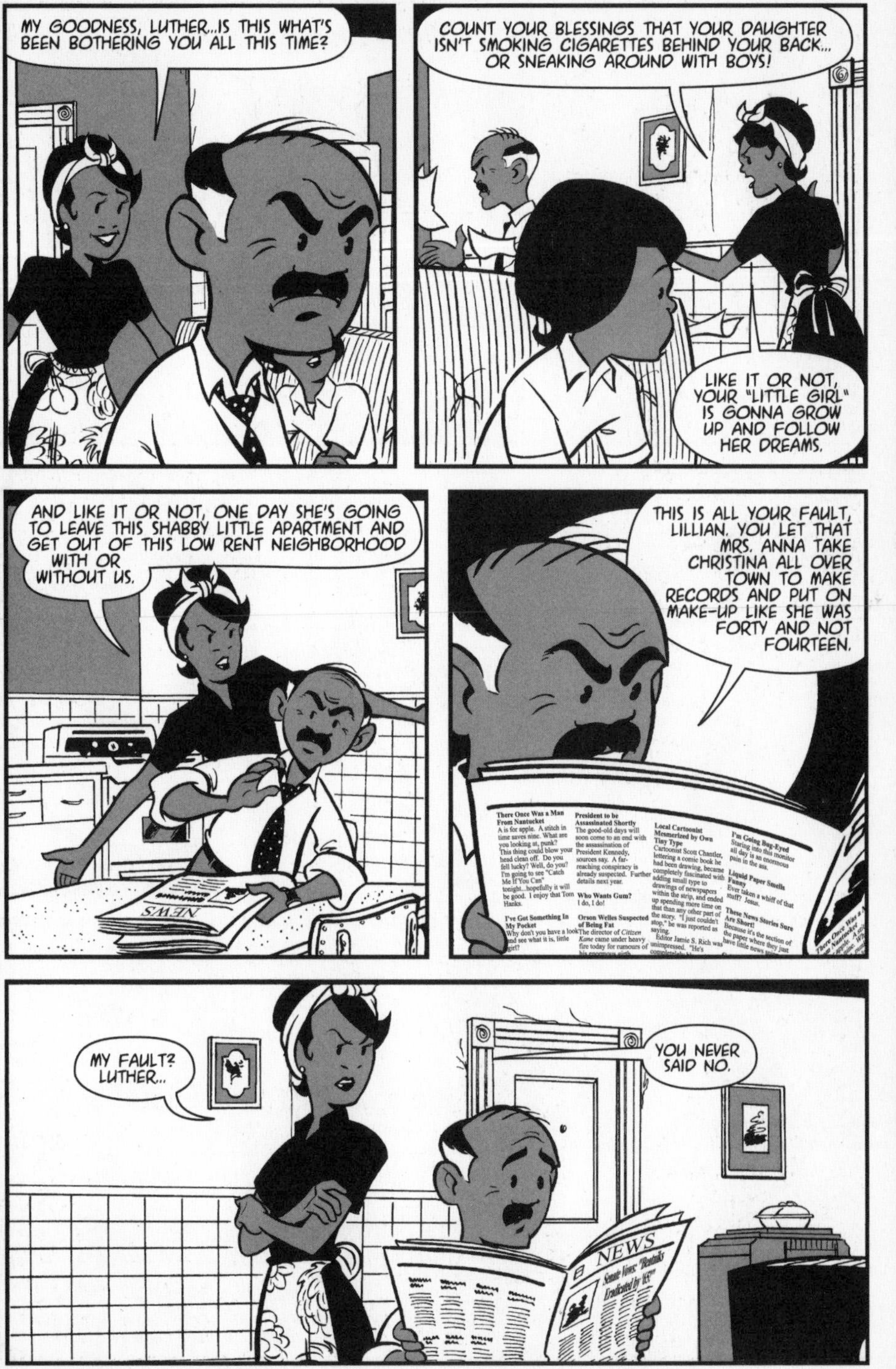
MY GOODNESS, LUTHER...IS THIS WHAT'S BEEN BOTHERING YOU ALL THIS TIME?
COUNT YOUR BLESSINGS THAT YOUR DAUGHTER ISN'T SMOKING CIGARETTES BEHIND YOUR BACK... OR SNEAKING AROUND WITH BOYS!
LIKE IT OR NOT, YOUR "LITTLE GIRL" IS GONNA GROW UP AND FOLLOW HER DREAMS.
AND LIKE IT OR NOT, ONE DAY SHE'S GOING TO LEAVE THIS SHABBY LITTLE APARTMENT AND GET OUT OF THIS LOW RENT NEIGHBORHOOD WITH OR WITHOUT US.
NEWS
THIS IS ALL YOUR FAULT, LILLIAN. YOU LET THAT MRS. ANNA TAKE CHRISTINA ALL OVER TOWN TO MAKE RECORDS AND PUT ON MAKE-UP LIKE SHE WAS FORTY AND NOT FOURTEEN.
There Once Was a Man From Nantucket
A is for apple. A stitch in time saves nine. What are you looking at, punk? This thing could blow your head clean off. Do you fell lucky? Well, do you? I'm going to see "Catch Me If You Can" tonight...hopefully it will be good. I enjoy that Tom Hanks.
I've Got Something In My Pocket
Why don't you have a look and see what it is, little girl?
President to be Assassinated Shortly
The good-old days will soon come to an end with the assassination of President Kennedy, sources say. A far-reaching conspiracy is already suspected. Further details next year.
Who Wants Gum?
I do, I do!
Orson Welles Suspected of Being Fat
The director of Citizen Kane came under heavy fire today for rumours of
Local Cartoonist Mesmerized by Own Tiny Type
Cartoonist Scott Chantler, lettering a comic book he had been drawing, became completely fascinated with adding small type to drawings of newspapers within the strip, and ended up spending more time on that than any other part of the story. "I just couldn't stop," he was reported as saying.
Editor Jamie S. Rich was unimpressed. "He's
I'm Going Bug-Eyed
Staring into this monitor all day is an enormous pain in the ass.
Liquid Paper Smells Funny
Ever taken a whiff of that stuff? Jesus.
These News Stories Sure Are Short!
Because it's the section of the paper where they just have little news
MY FAULT? LUTHER...
YOU NEVER SAID NO.
NEWS
Senate Vows: "Beatniks Eradicated by '65"

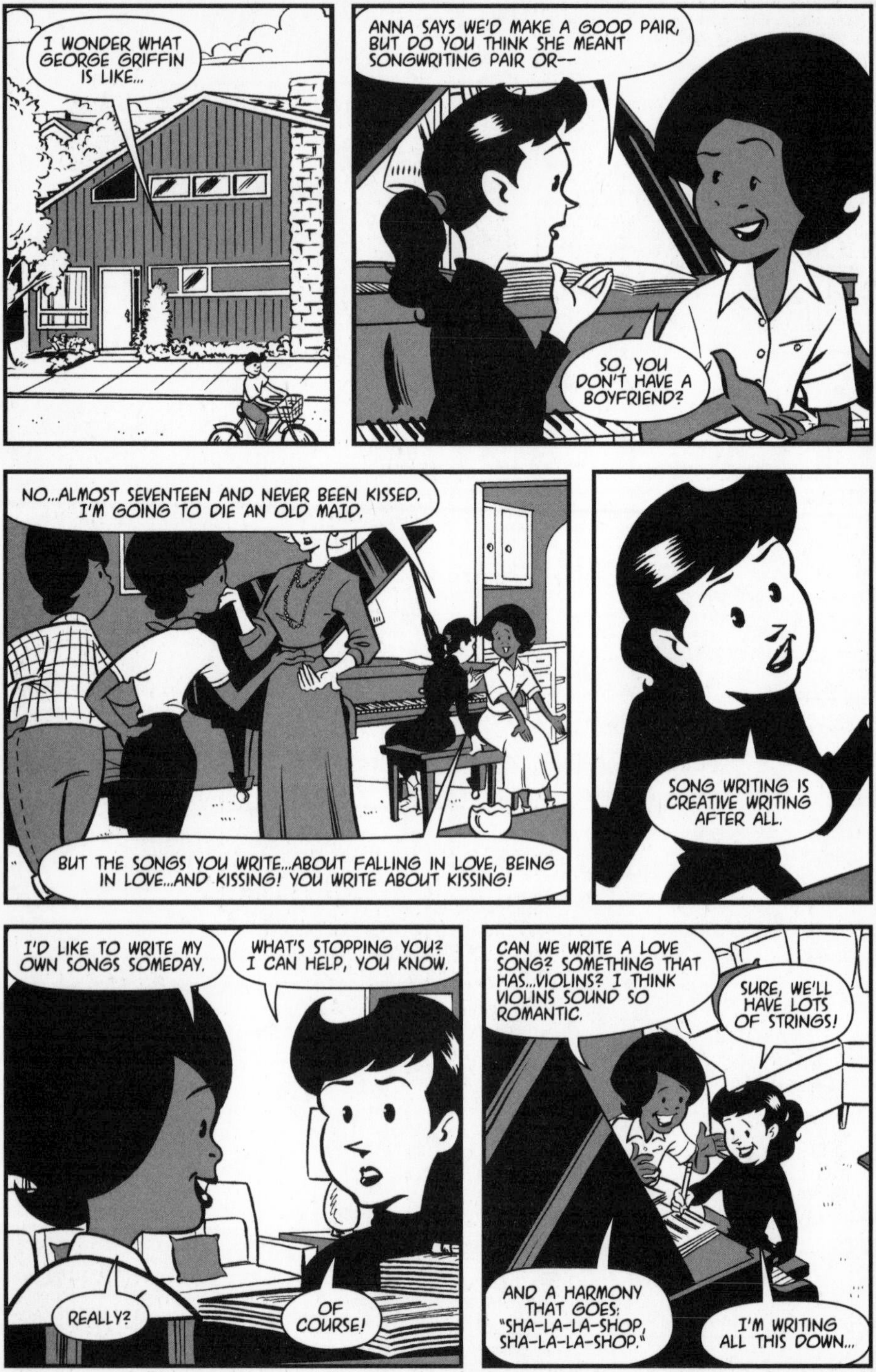
I WONDER WHAT GEORGE GRIFFIN IS LIKE...
ANNA SAYS WE'D MAKE A GOOD PAIR, BUT DO YOU THINK SHE MEANT SONGWRITING PAIR OR--
SO, YOU DON'T HAVE A BOYFRIEND?
NO...ALMOST SEVENTEEN AND NEVER BEEN KISSED. I'M GOING TO DIE AN OLD MAID.
BUT THE SONGS YOU WRITE...ABOUT FALLING IN LOVE, BEING IN LOVE...AND KISSING! YOU WRITE ABOUT KISSING!
SONG WRITING IS CREATIVE WRITING AFTER ALL.
I'D LIKE TO WRITE MY OWN SONGS SOMEDAY.
WHAT'S STOPPING YOU? I CAN HELP, YOU KNOW.
REALLY?
OF COURSE!
CAN WE WRITE A LOVE SONG? SOMETHING THAT HAS...VIOLINS? I THINK VIOLINS SOUND SO ROMANTIC.
SURE, WE'LL HAVE LOTS OF STRINGS!
AND A HARMONY THAT GOES: "SHA-LA-LA-SHOP, SHA-LA-LA-SHOP."
I'M WRITING ALL THIS DOWN...

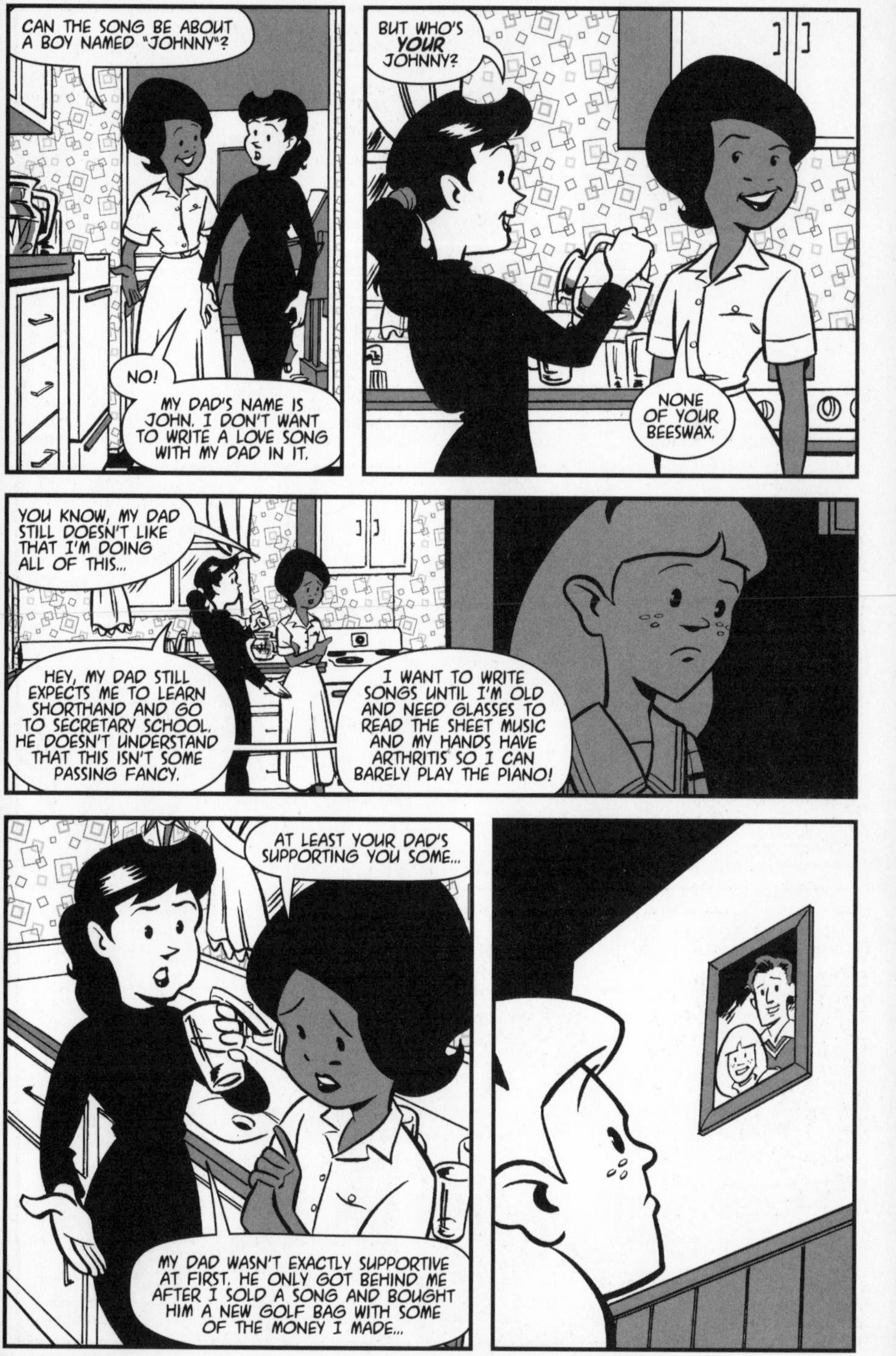
CAN THE SONG BE ABOUT A BOY NAMED "JOHNNY"?
NO!
MY DAD'S NAME IS JOHN. I DON'T WANT TO WRITE A LOVE SONG WITH MY DAD IN IT.
BUT WHO'S YOUR JOHNNY?
NONE OF YOUR BEESWAX.
YOU KNOW, MY DAD STILL DOESN'T LIKE THAT I'M DOING ALL OF THIS...
HEY, MY DAD STILL EXPECTS ME TO LEARN SHORTHAND AND GO TO SECRETARY SCHOOL. HE DOESN'T UNDERSTAND THAT THIS ISN'T SOME PASSING FANCY.
I WANT TO WRITE SONGS UNTIL I'M OLD AND NEED GLASSES TO READ THE SHEET MUSIC AND MY HANDS HAVE ARTHRITIS SO I CAN BARELY PLAY THE PIANO!
AT LEAST YOUR DAD'S SUPPORTING YOU SOME...
MY DAD WASN'T EXACTLY SUPPORTIVE AT FIRST. HE ONLY GOT BEHIND ME AFTER I SOLD A SONG AND BOUGHT HIM A NEW GOLF BAG WITH SOME OF THE MONEY I MADE...

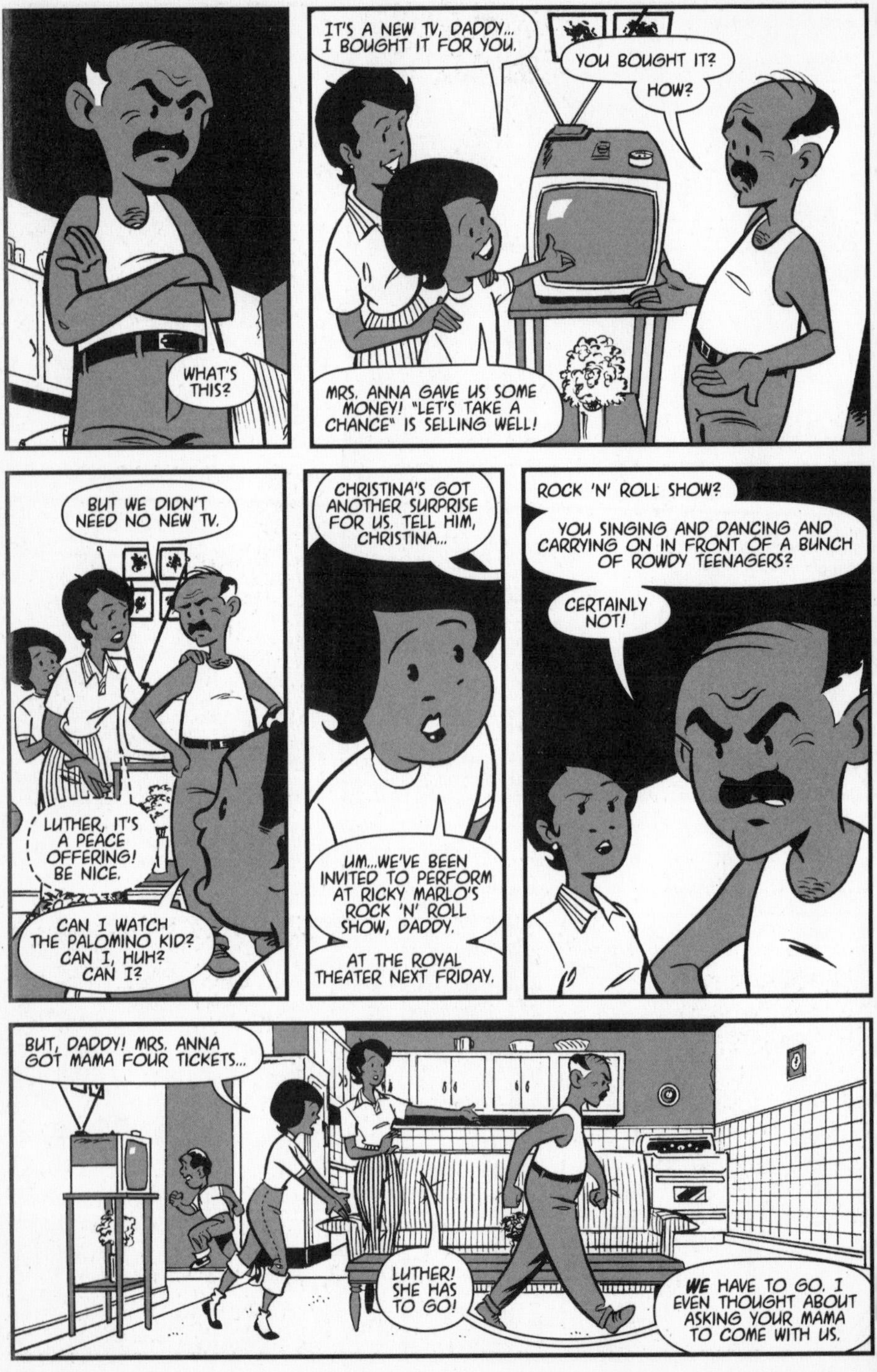
WHAT'S THIS?
IT'S A NEW TV, DADDY... I BOUGHT IT FOR YOU.
YOU BOUGHT IT?
HOW?
MRS. ANNA GAVE US SOME MONEY! "LET'S TAKE A CHANCE" IS SELLING WELL!
BUT WE DIDN'T NEED NO NEW TV.
LUTHER, IT'S A PEACE OFFERING! BE NICE.
CAN I WATCH THE PALOMINO KID? CAN I, HUH? CAN I?
CHRISTINA'S GOT ANOTHER SURPRISE FOR US. TELL HIM, CHRISTINA...
UM...WE'VE BEEN INVITED TO PERFORM AT RICKY MARLO'S ROCK 'N' ROLL SHOW, DADDY.
AT THE ROYAL THEATER NEXT FRIDAY.
ROCK 'N' ROLL SHOW?
YOU SINGING AND DANCING AND CARRYING ON IN FRONT OF A BUNCH OF ROWDY TEENAGERS?
CERTAINLY NOT!
BUT, DADDY! MRS. ANNA GOT MAMA FOUR TICKETS...
LUTHER! SHE HAS TO GO!
WE HAVE TO GO. I EVEN THOUGHT ABOUT ASKING YOUR MAMA TO COME WITH US.

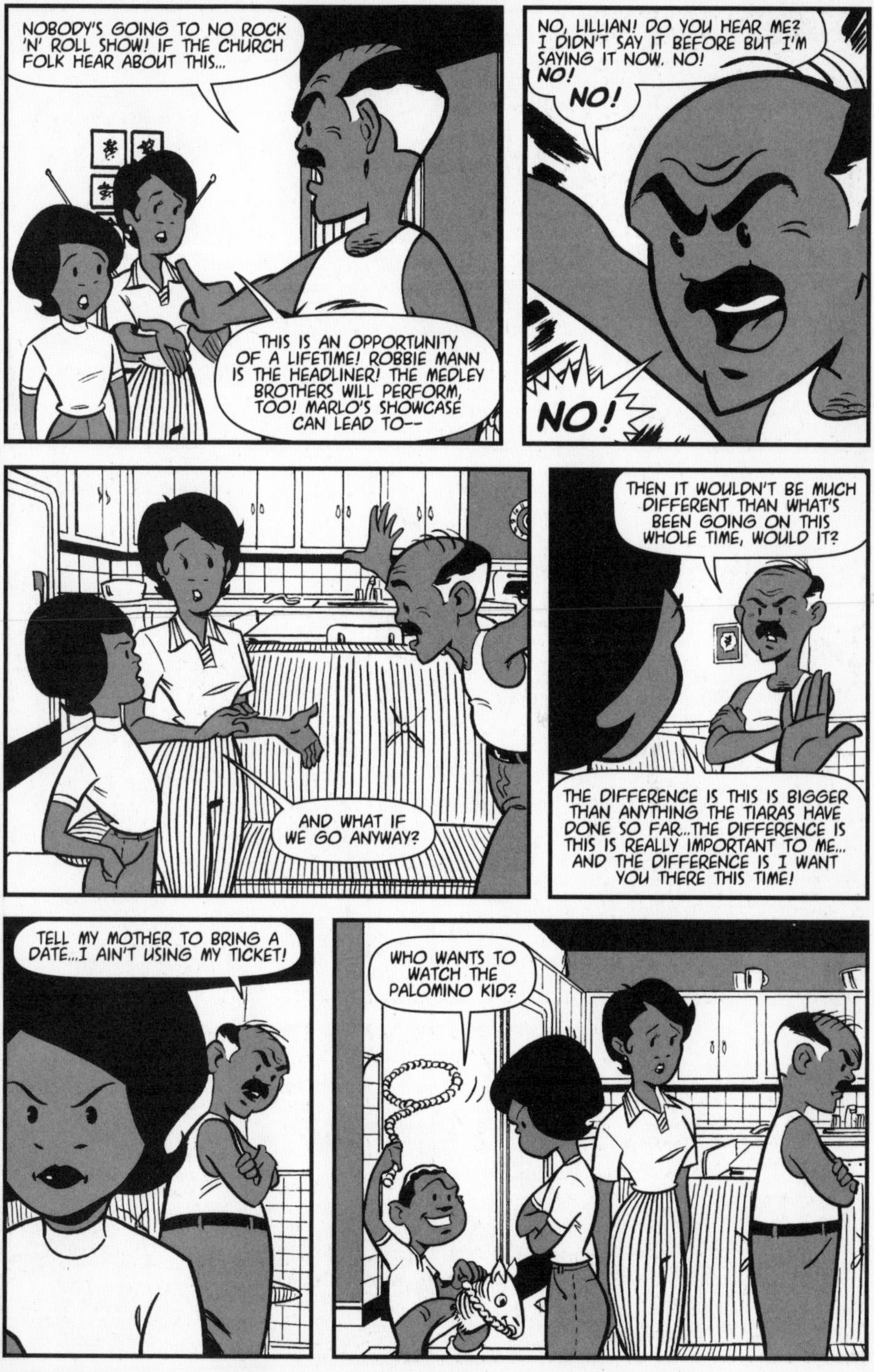

NOBODY'S GOING TO NO ROCK 'N' ROLL SHOW! IF THE CHURCH FOLK HEAR ABOUT THIS...
THIS IS AN OPPORTUNITY OF A LIFETIME! ROBBIE MANN IS THE HEADLINER! THE MEDLEY BROTHERS WILL PERFORM, TOO! MARLO'S SHOWCASE CAN LEAD TO--
NO, LILLIAN! DO YOU HEAR ME? I DIDN'T SAY IT BEFORE BUT I'M SAYING IT NOW. NO! NO!
NO!
NO!
AND WHAT IF WE GO ANYWAY?
THEN IT WOULDN'T BE MUCH DIFFERENT THAN WHAT'S BEEN GOING ON THIS WHOLE TIME, WOULD IT?
THE DIFFERENCE IS THIS IS BIGGER THAN ANYTHING THE TIARAS HAVE DONE SO FAR...THE DIFFERENCE IS THIS IS REALLY IMPORTANT TO ME... AND THE DIFFERENCE IS I WANT YOU THERE THIS TIME!
TELL MY MOTHER TO BRING A DATE...I AIN'T USING MY TICKET!
WHO WANTS TO WATCH THE PALOMINO KID?

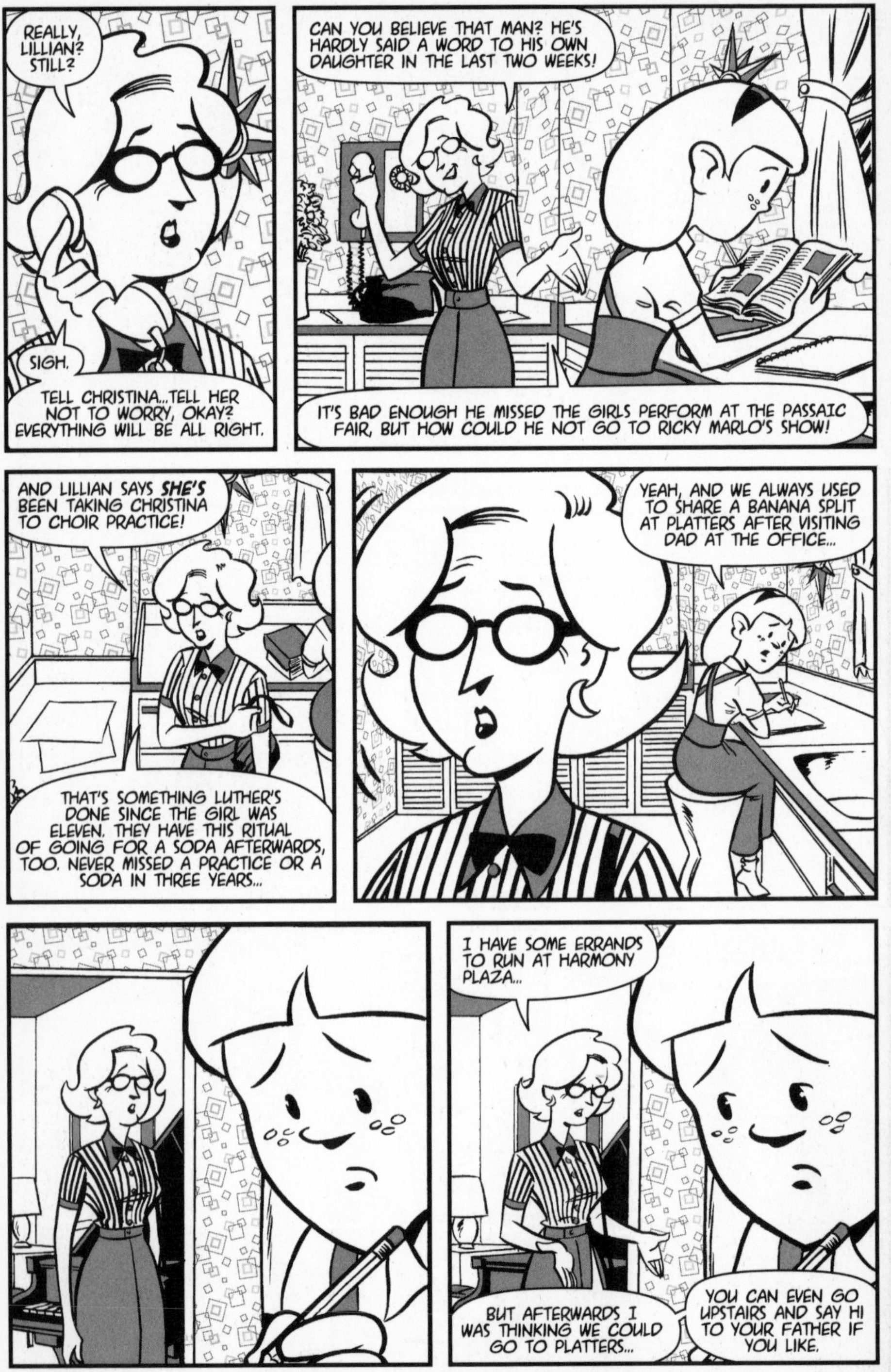
REALLY, LILLIAN? STILL?
SIGH.
TELL CHRISTINA...TELL HER NOT TO WORRY, OKAY? EVERYTHING WILL BE ALL RIGHT.
CAN YOU BELIEVE THAT MAN? HE'S HARDLY SAID A WORD TO HIS OWN DAUGHTER IN THE LAST TWO WEEKS!
IT'S BAD ENOUGH HE MISSED THE GIRLS PERFORM AT THE PASSAIC FAIR, BUT HOW COULD HE NOT GO TO RICKY MARLO'S SHOW!
AND LILLIAN SAYS ***SHE'S*** BEEN TAKING CHRISTINA TO CHOIR PRACTICE!
THAT'S SOMETHING LUTHER'S DONE SINCE THE GIRL WAS ELEVEN. THEY HAVE THIS RITUAL OF GOING FOR A SODA AFTERWARDS, TOO. NEVER MISSED A PRACTICE OR A SODA IN THREE YEARS...
YEAH, AND WE ALWAYS USED TO SHARE A BANANA SPLIT AT PLATTERS AFTER VISITING DAD AT THE OFFICE...
I HAVE SOME ERRANDS TO RUN AT HARMONY PLAZA...
BUT AFTERWARDS I WAS THINKING WE COULD GO TO PLATTERS...
YOU CAN EVEN GO UPSTAIRS AND SAY HI TO YOUR FATHER IF YOU LIKE.

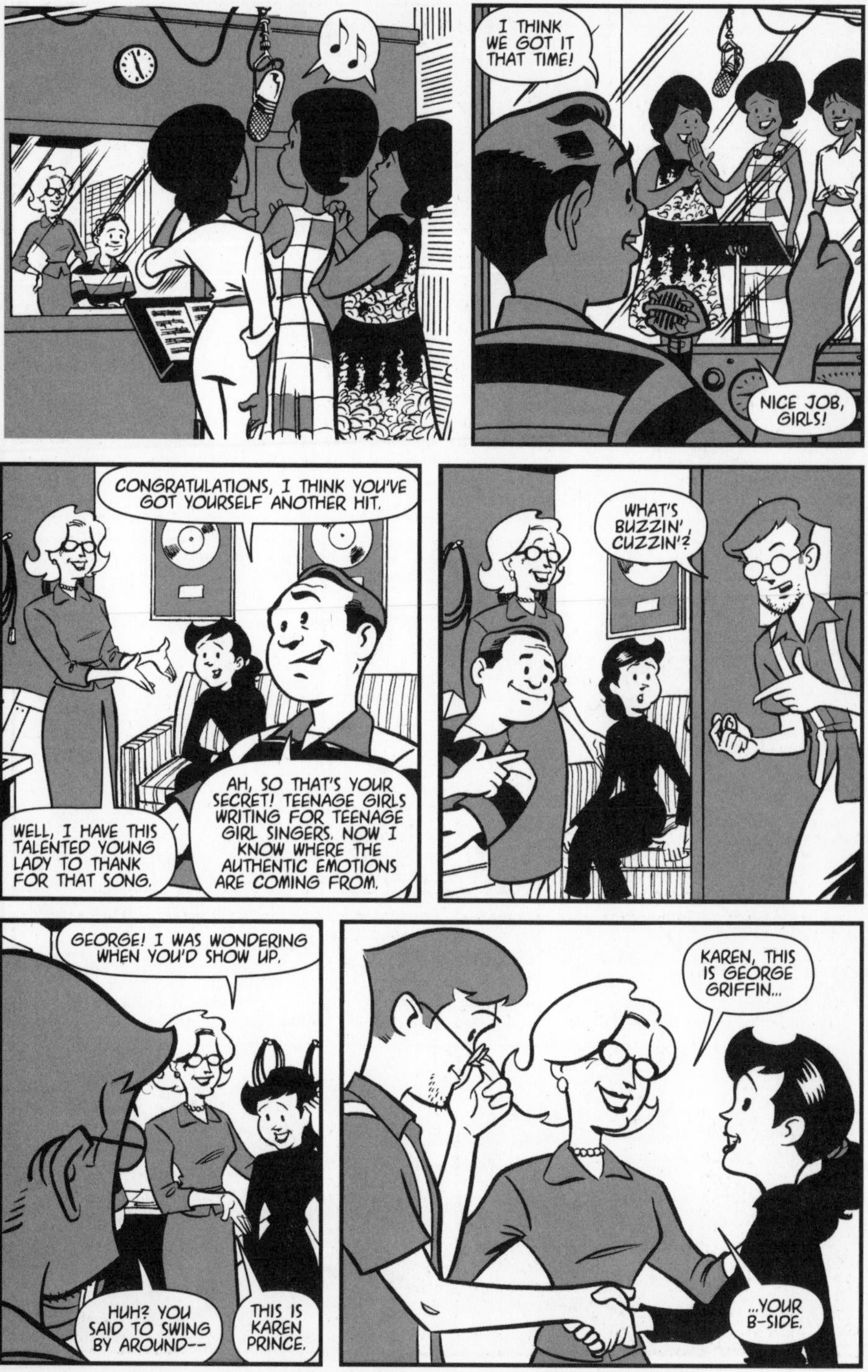
I THINK WE GOT IT THAT TIME!
NICE JOB, GIRLS!
CONGRATULATIONS, I THINK YOU'VE GOT YOURSELF ANOTHER HIT.
WELL, I HAVE THIS TALENTED YOUNG LADY TO THANK FOR THAT SONG.
AH, SO THAT'S YOUR SECRET! TEENAGE GIRLS WRITING FOR TEENAGE GIRL SINGERS. NOW I KNOW WHERE THE AUTHENTIC EMOTIONS ARE COMING FROM.
WHAT'S BUZZIN', CUZZIN'?
GEORGE! I WAS WONDERING WHEN YOU'D SHOW UP.
HUH? YOU SAID TO SWING BY AROUND--
THIS IS KAREN PRINCE.
KAREN, THIS IS GEORGE GRIFFIN...
...YOUR B-SIDE.

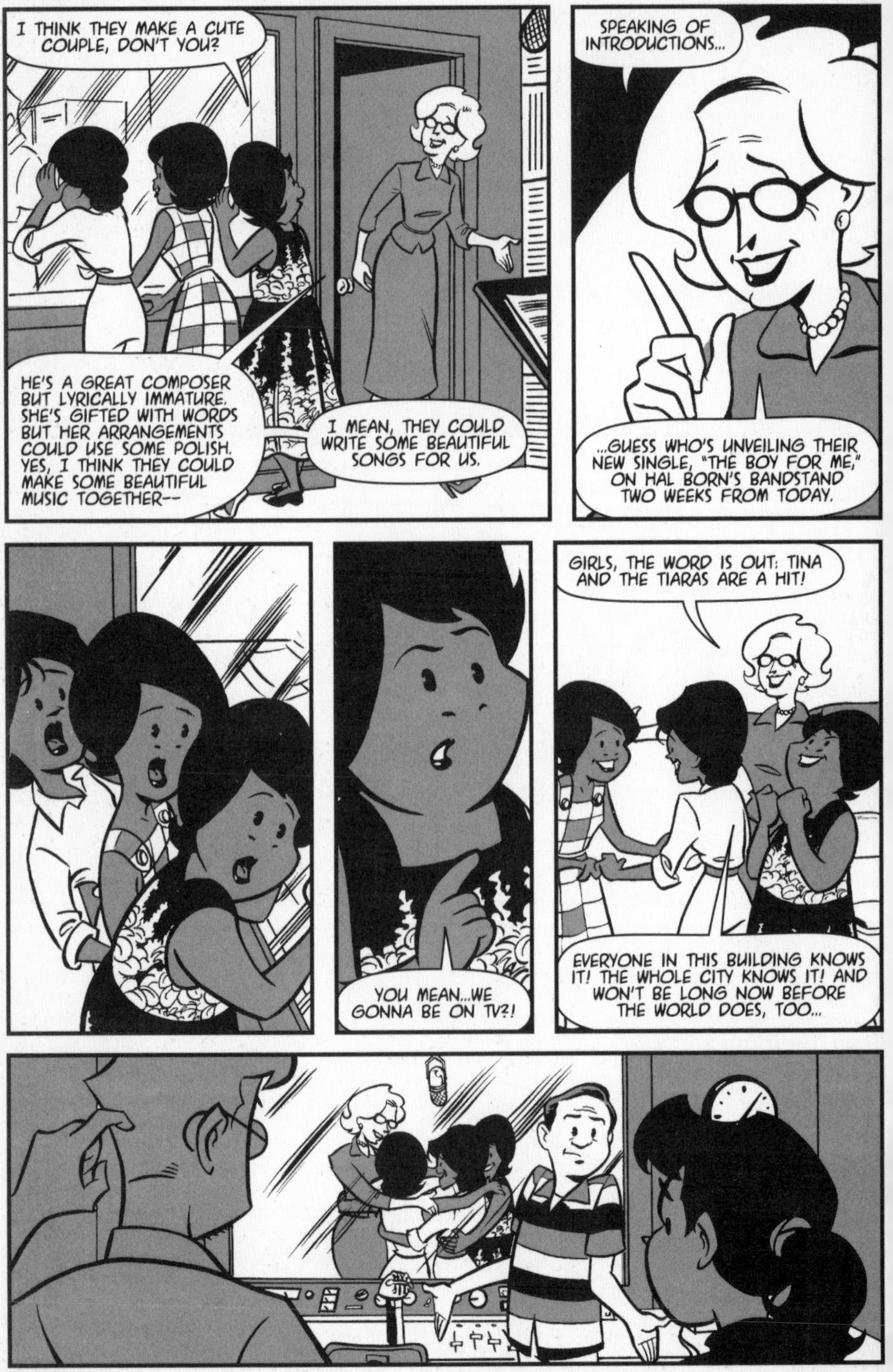
I THINK THEY MAKE A CUTE COUPLE, DON'T YOU?
HE'S A GREAT COMPOSER BUT LYRICALLY IMMATURE. SHE'S GIFTED WITH WORDS BUT HER ARRANGEMENTS COULD USE SOME POLISH. YES, I THINK THEY COULD MAKE SOME BEAUTIFUL MUSIC TOGETHER--
I MEAN, THEY COULD WRITE SOME BEAUTIFUL SONGS FOR US.
SPEAKING OF INTRODUCTIONS...
...GUESS WHO'S UNVEILING THEIR NEW SINGLE, "THE BOY FOR ME," ON HAL BORN'S BANDSTAND TWO WEEKS FROM TODAY.
YOU MEAN...WE GONNA BE ON TV?!
GIRLS, THE WORD IS OUT: TINA AND THE TIARAS ARE A HIT!
EVERYONE IN THIS BUILDING KNOWS IT! THE WHOLE CITY KNOWS IT! AND WON'T BE LONG NOW BEFORE THE WORLD DOES, TOO...

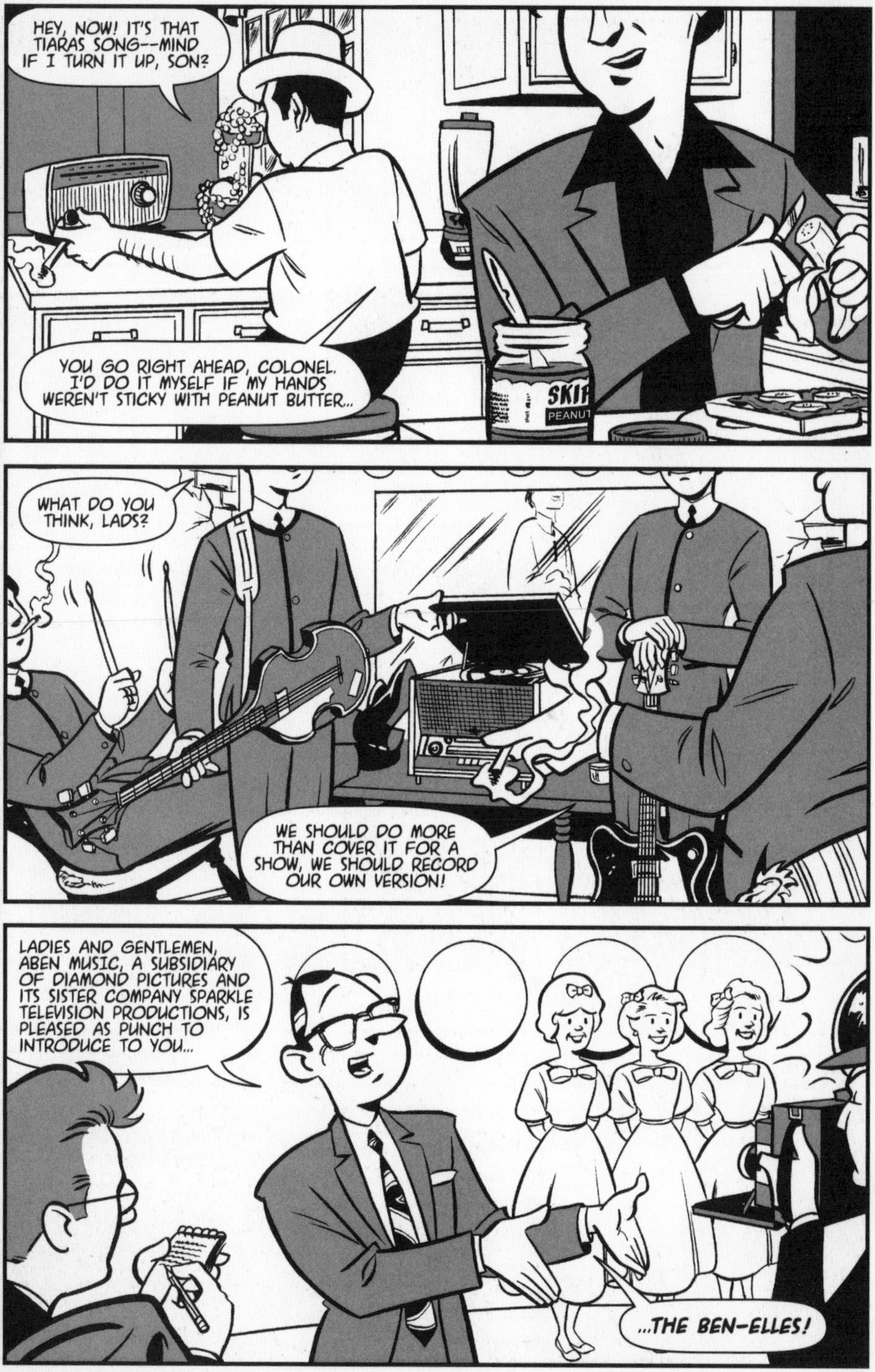
HEY, NOW! IT'S THAT TIARAS SONG--MIND IF I TURN IT UP, SON?
YOU GO RIGHT AHEAD, COLONEL. I'D DO IT MYSELF IF MY HANDS WEREN'T STICKY WITH PEANUT BUTTER...
SKIP PEANUT
WHAT DO YOU THINK, LADS?
WE SHOULD DO MORE THAN COVER IT FOR A SHOW, WE SHOULD RECORD OUR OWN VERSION!
LADIES AND GENTLEMEN, ABEN MUSIC, A SUBSIDIARY OF DIAMOND PICTURES AND ITS SISTER COMPANY SPARKLE TELEVISION PRODUCTIONS, IS PLEASED AS PUNCH TO INTRODUCE TO YOU...
...THE BEN-ELLES!

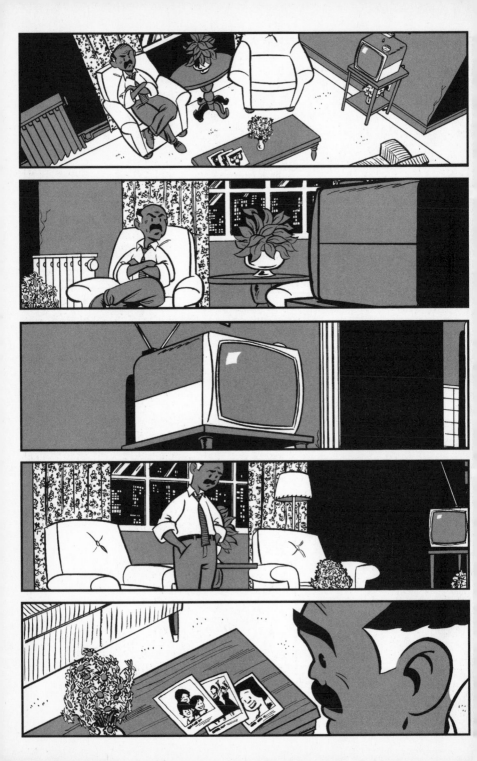

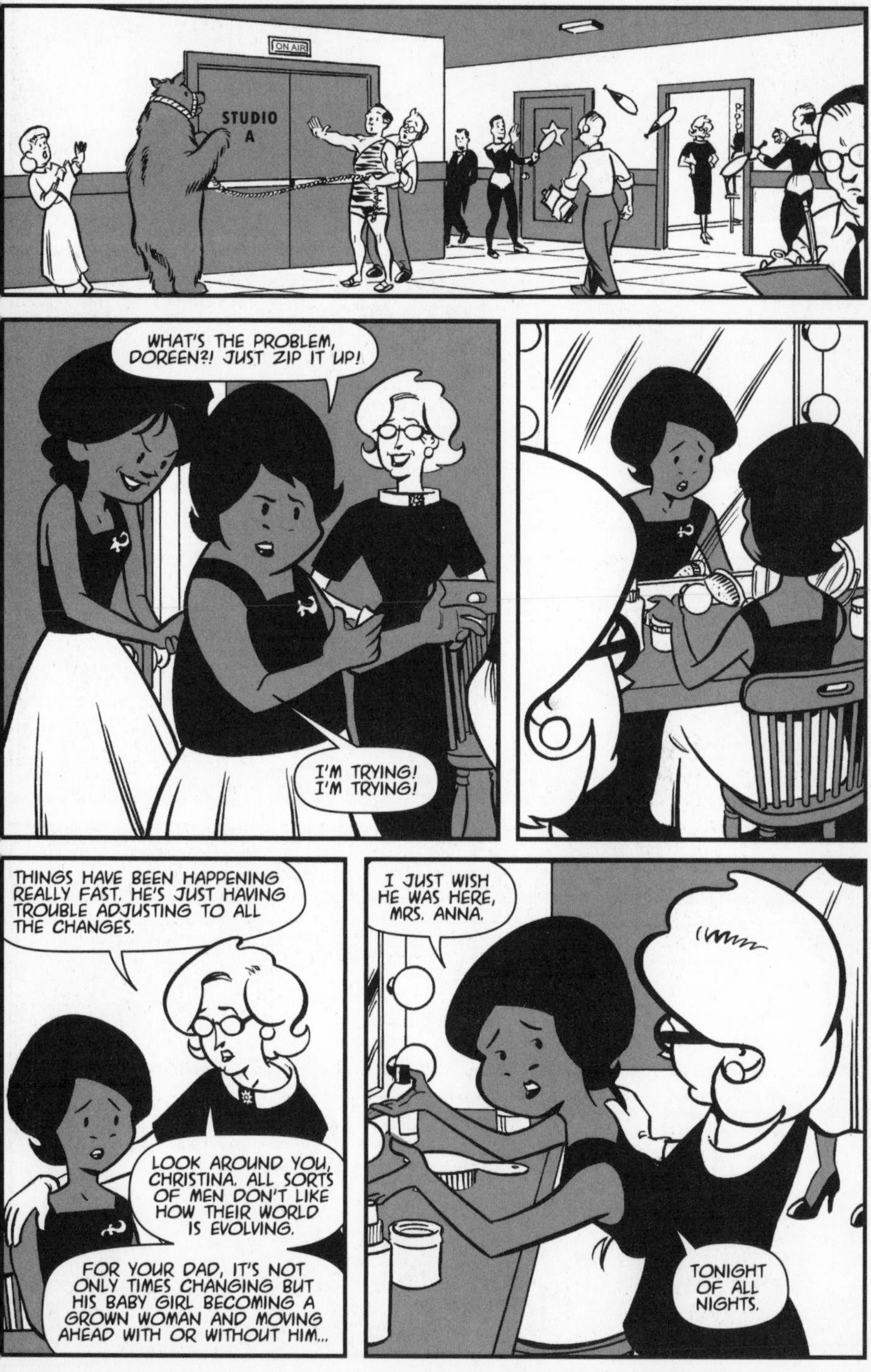
ON AIR
STUDIO A
WHAT'S THE PROBLEM, DOREEN?! JUST ZIP IT UP!
I'M TRYING! I'M TRYING!
THINGS HAVE BEEN HAPPENING REALLY FAST. HE'S JUST HAVING TROUBLE ADJUSTING TO ALL THE CHANGES.
LOOK AROUND YOU, CHRISTINA. ALL SORTS OF MEN DON'T LIKE HOW THEIR WORLD IS EVOLVING.
FOR YOUR DAD, IT'S NOT ONLY TIMES CHANGING BUT HIS BABY GIRL BECOMING A GROWN WOMAN AND MOVING AHEAD WITH OR WITHOUT HIM...
I JUST WISH HE WAS HERE, MRS. ANNA.
TONIGHT OF ALL NIGHTS.

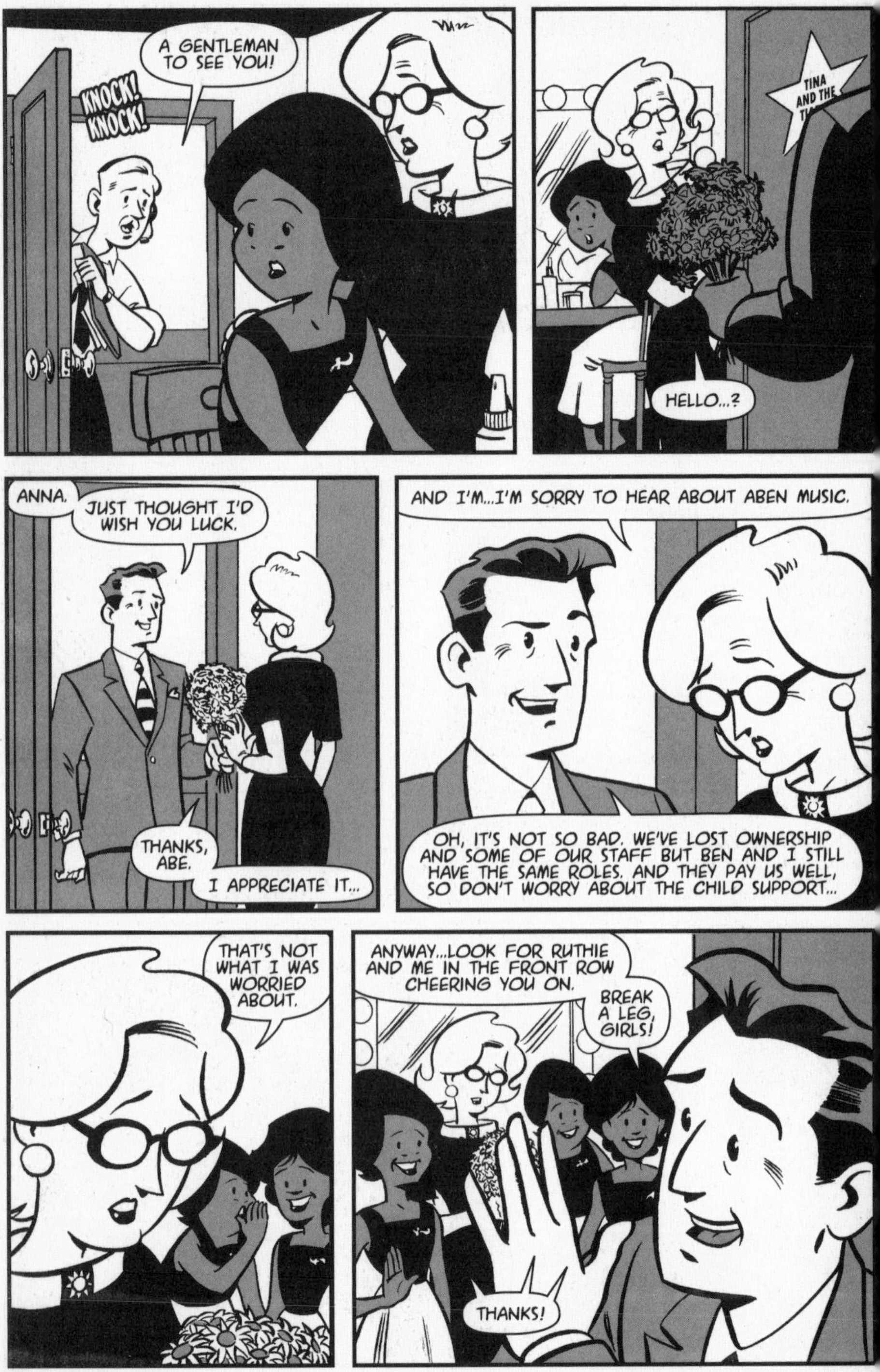
KNOCK! KNOCK!
A GENTLEMAN TO SEE YOU!
TINA AND THE
HELLO...?
ANNA.
JUST THOUGHT I'D WISH YOU LUCK.
THANKS, ABE.
I APPRECIATE IT...
AND I'M...I'M SORRY TO HEAR ABOUT ABEN MUSIC.
OH, IT'S NOT SO BAD. WE'VE LOST OWNERSHIP AND SOME OF OUR STAFF BUT BEN AND I STILL HAVE THE SAME ROLES. AND THEY PAY US WELL, SO DON'T WORRY ABOUT THE CHILD SUPPORT...
THAT'S NOT WHAT I WAS WORRIED ABOUT.
ANYWAY...LOOK FOR RUTHIE AND ME IN THE FRONT ROW CHEERING YOU ON.
BREAK A LEG, GIRLS!
THANKS!

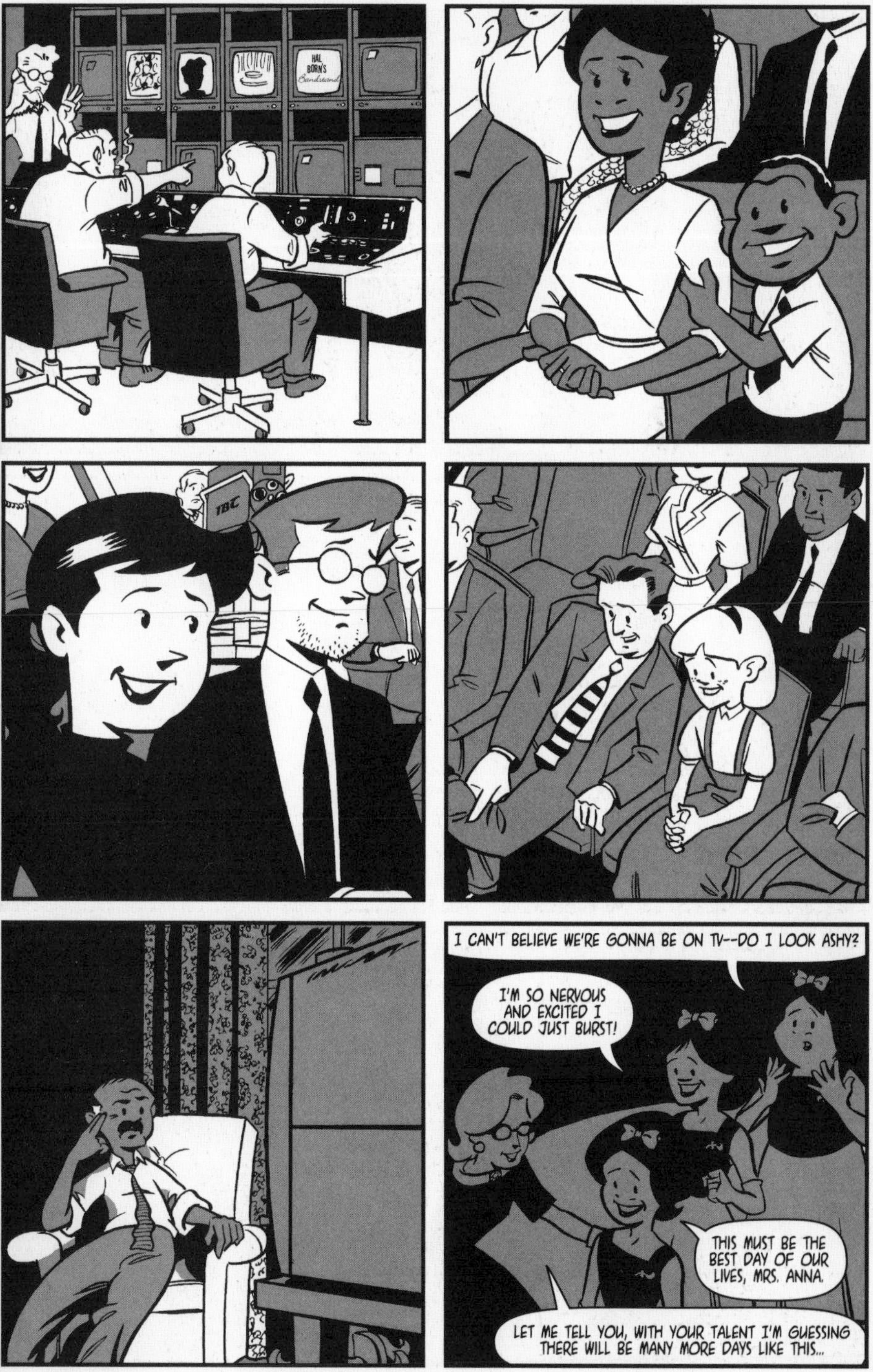
HAL BORN'S Bandstand
IBC
I CAN'T BELIEVE WE'RE GONNA BE ON TV--DO I LOOK ASHY?
I'M SO NERVOUS AND EXCITED I COULD JUST BURST!
THIS MUST BE THE BEST DAY OF OUR LIVES, MRS. ANNA.
LET ME TELL YOU, WITH YOUR TALENT I'M GUESSING THERE WILL BE MANY MORE DAYS LIKE THIS...

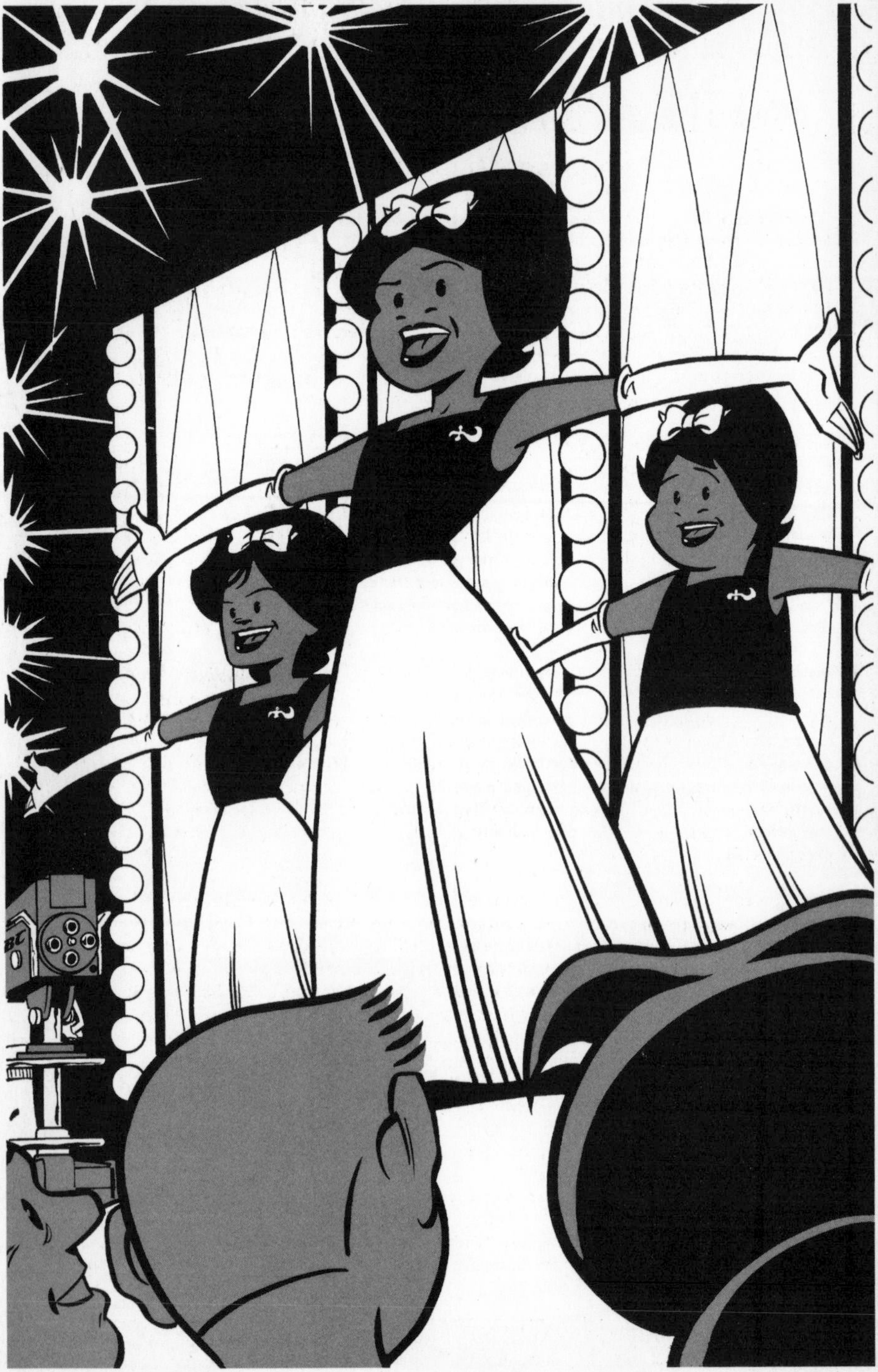

I HEAR A SYMPHONY...

An afterword by Jamie S. Rich

When one considers the girl groups of the 1960s—vocal outfits like The Shirelles, The Chiffons, and The Ronnettes—it's amazing to realize how cynical about pop music we've become.

Right now, we're in the death throes of the second generation of boy bands (at least in North America; in Europe, they never fully gave up the ghost to the tedium of early '90s earnestness). Modern groups like N*Sync and the Backstreet Boys were greeted with distrusting ears and gripes about record companies putting them together and other people writing their songs. Plus, they were seen as a phenomenon suitable only for teenage girls. God forbid adults listen to them, and should a teenage boy wish to emulate Nick Carter, he'd likely be beat-up by a shirtless cad with his boxers showing that thinks he's DMX.

But back in the era of the Brill Building, when the three-minute pop song ruled the radio, there was no such grumbling. In fact, when some neophyte serious music fan extols the virtue of the latest off-key loser to score a record deal, praising him for recording his own material, I tend to remind said *High Fidelity*-wannabe that a lot of the revered records that came out of Motown were just as much the products of writers and producers as they were the performers, and The Beatles began as a covers band. Hell, even Jimi Hendrix had one of his biggest hits singing Bob Dylan. Writing your own material isn't all it's cracked up to be. That's how we end up with wankers like Jon Mayer or art school dropouts like The Flaming Lips. (I heard a gasp from the boy in the turtleneck in the back. He can't believe I would lump both of those acts into the same diss. Surely the Lips deserve a kicking with a completely different set of boots than Mayer, he believes.)

Groups were formed however groups were formed. Sometimes they were friends singing doo wop on a street corner, catching the ears of the right person. The Crystals, who had hits like "Da Doo Ron Ron" and "He's A Rebel," started off winning a high school talent show. The Shirelles, who brought us "Will You Still Love Me Tomorrow?" and "Solider Boy," used to sing in the hallways until a fellow student, whose mom happened to have a record label, heard them. Often, a vocal group was a mix-and-match batch of singers that might have been hanging around that day. Perhaps the greatest benefactor of good luck was solo artist Little Eva, singer of "The Locomotion." She was the songwriters' babysitter and just happened to be working the day they needed someone to sing on the demo. A little bit of happenstance can go a long way in the recording of a pop classic.

Little Eva's stumble upon glory came to be at the Brill Building. Probably the most famous hit factory of the era, the Brill Building was a place where a record could be written and recorded and sent to the charts in the course of a single day. It gave birth to a ton of stellar 45s, to songs that hold a lasting impression even now, and also gave rise to bubblegum. It was here that Gerry Goffin met Carole King, and Barry Mann and Cynthia Weill wrote such hits as "I Love How You Love Me" and "Who Put the Bomp." So magic was the melodic touch of these four, their songs were often exported overseas so rock acts like The Animals could record them. Eric Burdon and the boys had no concerns about people branding them as fake because they took a song like "We Gotta Get Out of This Place" from pop composers—they knew a good tune was a good tune. (Decades later Bon Jovi would rediscover this formula, hiring Max Martin, the Swedish producer behind a lot of the Britney Spears and Backstreet Boys hits, to give them a comeback hit with "It's My Life." A tune is a tune.)

Not one flavor of song, nor one flavor of group.

Don't go kidding yourselves that this music was just some banal moneymaking vehicle, either. Sure, the same period produced hits by folks like The Righteous Brothers that pretty much were all surface—surface polished by feeling, but surface nonetheless. "Unchained Melody" is a lovesong with a tinge of sexual hunger, but it's still primarily a lovesong. The women weren't so shy...but they were more coy. King's "Will

You Still Love Me Tomorrow?" was, when broken down, a song sung by a girl about to sleep with her man who was worried that he'd no longer respect her in the morning. The Supremes had "Love Child," which was just what the title suggests—a song about the product of an illicit affair. And let's not even go into the strange politics of the Phil Spector-penned "hit" for The Crystals—"He Hit Me (It Felt Like a Kiss)."

And the sexuality wasn't just between the lines of the songs, it was in the presentation, as well. Once again, this set the girl groups apart from their male contemporaries (at least before rock really took hold), and in particular, this was territory pioneered by The Ronettes. No boy wanted to be Bill Medley, but a girl might want to be Ronnie Spector, and while initially the Fab Four were suitable to bring home for milk and cookies, this trio seemed a little more dangerous. Paul McCartney's eyes said, "I'm cute and loveable," but The Ronettes looked like they were more than your average guy could handle. Even the names of some of the bands—The Flirtations, The Exciters, Candy & the Kisses—were saying these girls weren't that innocent long before Britney Spears was around to make the same protest.

It was a revolution of melody. You could be harmonizing on the street corner one day, topping the charts the next. The songs were universal enough to be specific to each person that heard them—which is the essence of pop, and is why the music endures to this day. Contemporary bands continue to find the music of the girl groups and reinterpret it. In recent memory, British rock group Travis recorded a rousing and tender-hearted version of "Be My Baby" for a single B-side (remember those?), and '80s synth-pop duo Erasure, on their 2003 album of covers, *Other People's Songs*, pillaged the Spector discography, most notably on a splendid run-through of The Ronettes classic "Walking In the Rain." (Despite his current legal troubles, Spector's work still retains its stunning genius.) Yeah, sure, we're all cynical and sophisticated and modern, and we think we have all the answers...but a tune is a tune. The power of pop music is to break through all that and remind us of our most basic emotions.

If you ever forget what makes life really important, the reasons that a heart beats inside your chest, all you need to do is remember the girl groups and the people who perfected this insidious method of aural manipulation. Put on "One Fine Day" or "I Hear a Symphony" and let them work their magic.

– Jamie S. Rich,
  wishing he never saw the sunshine
  February, 2003

FOR FURTHER EXPLORATION, MAY I RECOMMEND:

• Phil Spector, *Back To Mono* 4-CD box set (Abko Records, 1991)

• *Girl Groups: Fabulous Females That Rocked the World* by John Clemente (Krause Publications, 2000) – an alphabetical history from the 1950s up through the gorgeous Go-Go's

• *Bubblegum Music is the Naked Truth*, edited by Kim Cooper and David Smay (Feral House, 2001) – not so much a source of information on girl groups, but it does provide interesting insight on the transition from the classic Brill Building sound to the less substantial bubblegum period, including when the hit factory owned by Don Kirshner was sold to a movie studio, much like Aben Music in *Days Like This*

• http://www.mann-weil.com/thehits.html - the official website of two of the best Brill Building songwriters

• *The Songmakers* DVD and CD set – A&E Network's excellent documentary on the Brill Building

Jamie S. Rich, *in addition to being the editor-in-chief of Oni Press, is the writer of the music-inspired novel* Cut My Hair, *as well as a freelance music journalist and the former co-host of Portland, Oregon's premiere cable-access show about British pop music,* @lright. *Visit him at confessions123.com.*

BIOGROPHY

J. TORRES was a long-time comic book fan when he and artist Tim Levins released the debut issue of *The Copybook Tales* in 1996 as part of the burgeoning indie comics scene. Though much more downbeat slice-of-life and autobiographical comics were popular at the time, *The Copybook Tales* earned a dedicated following for its hopeful viewpoint and its take on the average comic book enthusiast's dream of becoming a professional creator. Torres followed this success with an eclectic list of creator-owned projects – like *Sidekicks*; *Alison Dare, Little Miss Adventures*; and *Jason & the Argobots* – and freelance gigs – Marvel's *Black Panther* and *X-Men: Ronin*; Tokyopop's *Dragon Hunter*. *The Copybook Tales* has also been collected into book form by Oni Press.

Currently, Torres lives in Toronto where he spends his days writing several upcoming projects, including the second *Jason & the Argobots*, *Sparta*, and *Go Club*, a comic that will reunite him with Tim Levins. His nights are filled with a lot of socializing and trendsetting.

SCOTT CHANTLER was born on a frozen February morning in Deep River, Ontario, in 1972 and still hates the cold. After spending most of his childhood in St. Thomas, Ontario – a city best known for having run down Jumbo the elephant with a train – he moved to Waterloo, Ontario, where he studied Fine Arts and Film at the University of Waterloo. During his four years there, he created a popular comic strip for the student newspaper and had his works displayed in the University Gallery. By the time of his graduation in 1995, he had already embarked on a successful career as an illustrator and animator. His work has appeared in magazines, books, comics, and advertising for some of North America's most prestigious corporations. He recently completed his first animated short film, *Gone With the Wind in Sixty Seconds*.

Scott still lives in Waterloo, with his wife Shari and an excitable mutt named Cubby. When he isn't drawing, he enjoys movies, reading, history, canoe trips, poker games, jazz, and the occasional expensive cigar.

OTHER BOOKS FROM J. TORRES AND ONI PRESS...

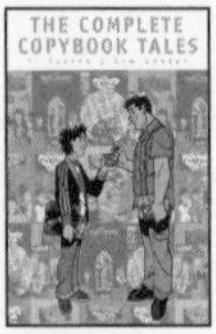
THE COMPLETE COPYBOOK TALES

THE COMPLETE COPYBOOK TALES™
by J. Torres & Tim Levins
240 pages black & white
$19.95 US, $29.95 Can
ISBN: 1-929998-20-1

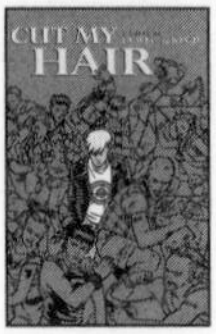
CUT MY HAIR

CUT MY HAIR™
by Jamie S. Rich
w/ Chynna Clugston-Major, Scott Morse, Judd Winick, & Andi Watson
236 pages, black-and-white text with illustrations
$15.95 US, $23.95 CAN
ISBN: 0-9700387-0-4

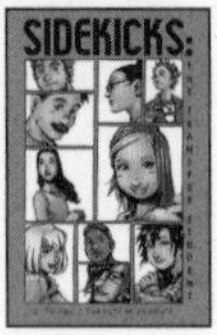
SIDEKICKS:

SIDEKICKS: THE TRANSFER STUDENT™
by J. Torres & Takeshi Miyazawa
104 pages, black-and-white interiors
$8.95 US, $12.95 US
ISBN 1-929998-40-6

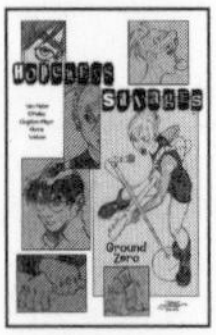
Ground Zero

HOPELESS SAVAGES: GROUND ZERO™
by Jen Van Meter & Bryan O'Malley
w/ Chynna Clugston-Major, Christine Norrie, & Andi Watson
128 pages black-and-white interiors
$11.95 US, $17.95 CAN
ISBN: 1-0200008-52-X

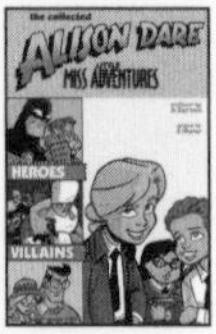
ALISON DARE
HEROES
VILLAINS

THE COLLECTED ALISON DARE™
by J. Torres & J. Bone
96 pages, black-and-white interiors
$8.95 US, $12.95 US
ISBN 1-929998-20-1

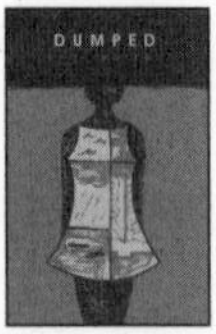
DUMPED

DUMPED™
by Andi Watson
56 pages, black-and-white interiors
$5.95 US, $9.95 Can
ISBN: 1-929998-41-4

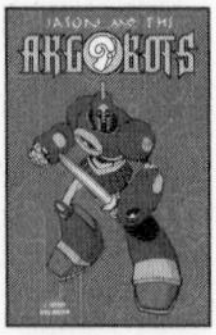
JASON AND THE
ARGOBOTS

JASON & THE ARGOBOTS VOL. I: BIRTHQUAKE™
by J. Torres & Mike Norton
112 pages, black-and-white interiors
$11.95 US, $17.95 CAN
ISBN: 1-929998-55-4
Available June, 2003

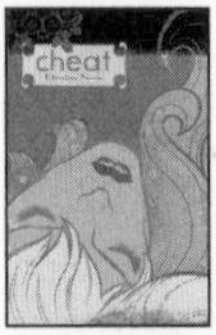
cheat

CHEAT™
by Christine Norrie
72 pages, black-and-white interiors
$5.95 US, $9.95 Can
ISBN: 1-929998-47-3

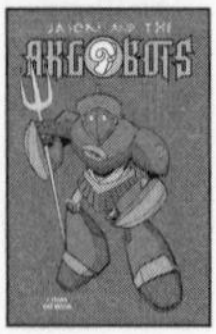
JASON AND THE
ARGOBOTS

JASON & THE ARGOBOTS, VOL. 2: MACHINA EX DEUS™
by J. Torres & Mike Norton
104 pages, black-and-white interiors
$10.95 US, $16.95 CAN
ISBN: 1-929998-56-2
Available August, 2003

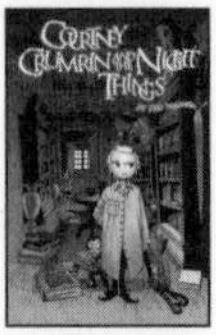
COURTNEY CRUMRIN AND THE NIGHT THINGS

COURTNEY CRUMRIN & THE NIGHT THINGS™
by Ted Naifeh
128 pages, black-and-white interiors
$11.95 US, $17.95 CAN
ISBN: 1-929998-42-2

Oni Press graphic novels are available at finer comics shops everywhere. For a comics store near you, call 1-888-COMIC-BOOK, or visit www.the-master-list.com.